THINKING

SCIENTIFICALLY

ABOUT

CONTROVERSIAL ISSUES

CLONES, CATS, AND CHEMICALS

NSTA PRESS

NATIONAL SCIENCE TEACHERS ASSOCIATION

Arlington, Virginia

NSTA PRESS
NATIONAL SCIENCE TEACHERS ASSOCIATION

Claire Reinburg, Director
J. Andrew Cocke, Associate Editor
Judy Cusick, Associate Editor
Betty Smith, Associate Editor

ART AND DESIGN Linda Olliver, Director
PRINTING AND PRODUCTION Catherine Lorrain-Hale, Director
   Nguyet Tran, Assistant Production Manager
   Jack Parker, Desktop Publishing Specialist
COVER DESIGN Linda Olliver, images from Getty, Photodisc, and BrandX

NATIONAL SCIENCE TEACHERS ASSOCIATION
Gerald F. Wheeler, Executive Director
David Beacom, Publisher

Library of Congress Cataloging-in-Publication Data

Slesnick, Irwin L.
  Clones, cats, and chemicals : thinking scientifically about controversial issues / by Irwin L. Slesnick.
    p. cm.
  Includes index.
  ISBN 0-87355-237-7
 1. Medical genetics. 2. Science—Public opinion. 3. Cats. 4. Games of chance (Mathematics) 5. Hunting. 6. Manned space flight. 7. Violence in mass media. I. Title.
  RB155.S54 2004
  303.48'3—dc22

            2004013337

Contents

(t) teacher   (s) student

t teacher   **S** student

Introduction

Science and technology continue to advance human knowledge at a rapid—some say *too* rapid—pace, challenging accepted beliefs and spurring debate across many fields. Often, it seems scientific research is advancing faster than laws can be created to ensure it proceeds in a safe, humane manner. Human cloning, for example, ignites the passion of both experts and the general population on ethical, moral, religious, economic, and political grounds. All members of society are called upon to make decisions about their health, their recreation, how their actions can affect the environment, whether to play the lottery, whether to support manned or unmanned space flight, whether to seek genetic testing for babies, or how strictly to control violence in the media. These are the issues that are examined in *Clones, Cats, and Chemicals: Thinking Scientifically About Controversial Issues.*

The National Science Education Standards recommend that students have experience grappling with issues that society must ultimately resolve. This publication examines such issues in the fields of biology, chemistry, physics, Earth science, technology, and mathematics. Each issue is presented in two parts: The first part is written for the teacher and contains background on the science of the issue and presents alternative resolutions. The second part is written for the student and may be photocopied and distributed to the class. It includes a brief presentation of the issue and questions or activities to guide the student in the decision-making process.

Teachers should not feel restricted by the questions and activities of each issue, or by the limits of the background. The details of the science and the mood of society that impinge upon the issues change rapidly. For example, Korean researcher Hwang Woo Suk's announcement of having produced a clone of a human blastocyst occurred during the reading of these galley proofs. And President George W. Bush's sudden declaration of plans for a manned flight to Mars within 20 years added political clout to the seemingly stalled manned space program.

It is quite likely that in every school district there are issues that arouse greater interest and passion than do these. Following the format of the topics in this book, however, a resourceful teacher can collect the facts of a local issue and then present the issue to the students to discuss, investigate, and work toward a resolution.

The goal of this publication is to give the science student an opportunity to discuss and investigate the scientific and social issues of concern on a regular basis, and to learn to be comfortable with difficult decisions.

This book was originally published in a previous edition under the title *Real Science, Real Decisions*. I would like to acknowledge the contributions of Jal S. Parakh and John A. Miller, who co-authored some of the pieces in the first edition.

Irwin L. Slesnick
Professor of Biology
Western Washington University
Bellingham, Washington

NATIONAL SCIENCE TEACHERS ASSOCIATION

Here Come the Clones

The foot of a sea anemone holds the stalk of the animal to the rocks on a shoreline or to the inside glass walls of an aquarium. As the sea anemone slithers across the rock or glass surfaces, an observer may find that pieces of the tissue of the foot appear to be ripped off the body and adhere as debris to the trail of the slowly moving creature. When one examines these pieces of discarded tissue, at first, they seem to be ordinary adult body cells. But then they appear to change into embryonic cells. Soon the fragments of cells begin to develop and grow into individual sea anemones that are genetically identical to the parent. Zoologists call this natural kind of asexual reproduction *pedal laceration*. All offspring of the parent are clones as they share the same set of genes as the one parent.

Natural cloning is more common among plants. Clones of single parent plants can arise from bulbs, spores, stems, and leaves. Plant breeders may develop a superior variety of apple (Red Delicious) and then, by producing millions of genetically identical trees that grow identically delicious apples, establish a successful fruit market.

FIGURE 1

The cloning (pedal laceration) of a sea anemone

The sea anemone reproduces through the process of pedal laceration, also known as longitudinal fission. As the anemone moves, pieces of the foot break off and develop into genetically identical individuals, or clones. Pedal lacerations are best viewed on the underside of the sea anemone, on the glass wall of an aquarium, for example.

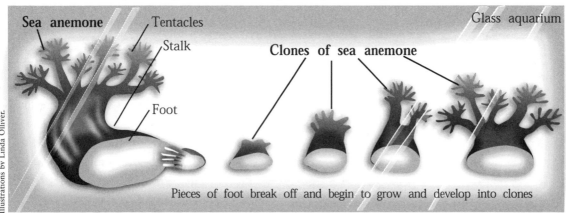

Illustrations by Linda Olliver.

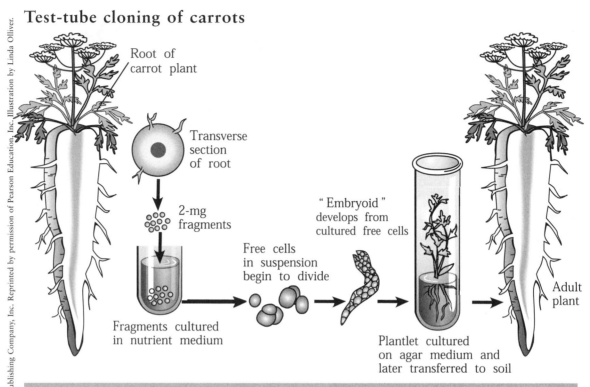

FIGURE 2

Test-tube cloning of carrots

Root of carrot plant

Transverse section of root

2-mg fragments

"Embryoid" develops from cultured free cells

Free cells in suspension begin to divide

Adult plant

Fragments cultured in nutrient medium

Plantlet cultured on agar medium and later transferred to soil

FIGURE 3

Nuclear transplantation

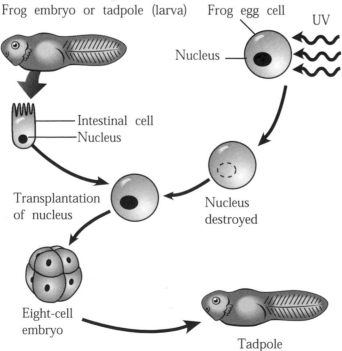

Frog embryo or tadpole (larva)

Frog egg cell

UV

Nucleus

Intestinal cell
Nucleus

Transplantation of nucleus

Nucleus destroyed

Eight-cell embryo

Tadpole

Well, it's only human nature to ask, "If sea anemones can clone themselves without hardly trying, and the natural cloning powers of plants are so easily exploited, why can't we begin learning how to clone ourselves?" The answer to that question is hidden in the secrets of the cell. All plants have one kind of cell that remains forever in the embryonic condition. These cell layers of embryonic tissue are totipotent and can give rise to new differentiated cells. Cut the stem of a plant and these cells will produce root, stem, and leaf tissues. In some animals, totipotent cells—as in the foot of a sea anemone—when cut, will dedifferentiate, and return to an embryonic condition. Then they

FIGURE 4

Cloning a mammal (Dolly the sheep)

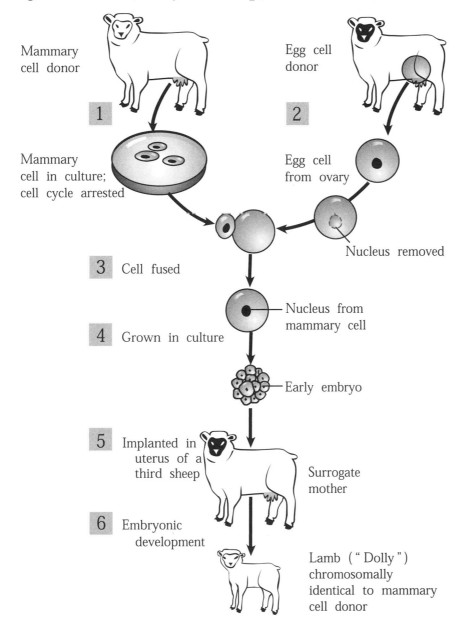

Mammary cell donor

Egg cell donor

1

2

Mammary cell in culture; cell cycle arrested

Egg cell from ovary

Nucleus removed

3 Cell fused

Nucleus from mammary cell

4 Grown in culture

Early embryo

5 Implanted in uterus of a third sheep

Surrogate mother

6 Embryonic development

Lamb ("Dolly") chromosomally identical to mammary cell donor

will redifferentiate into foot, muscle, and nerve tissue and the entire organism is cloned.

Could this natural cloning process be duplicated in the lab? At Cornell University in 1950, F. E. Stewart and his team of graduate students took tiny fragments from a fully differentiated root of a carrot and forced it to dedifferentiate into embryonic cells (an embryoid) and then redifferentiate into a fully adult carrot plant.

John Gurdon, a British biologist, pursued the next question: Can a differentiated cell from the intestine of a frog egg dedifferentiate and then redifferentiate into an adult frog? The result demonstrated in 1966 that the younger the totipotent donor cell, the greater the survival of the transplant.

In 1997, Scottish researcher Ian Wilmut and his team announced that they had cloned an adult sheep by transplanting the nucleus from an udder of a mammary gland of an adult sheep into an egg cell from another sheep. The cloned animal, named Dolly, was not identical to the donor mammary cell mother, as the mitochondrial DNA of the egg cell belonged to the egg cell donor. Techniques used by Wilmut to clone the sheep depended upon the breakthrough involved in starving the udder body cell of nutrients, thus interrupting the normal cycle of growth and division of the cell. In this quiet stage the cell can be reprogrammed to function as a newly fertilized egg.

Dolly bred twice, once giving birth to a ewe, and later having three lambs, a ewe and two rams.

Then in 1998, researchers in Hawaii announced that they had cloned 50 mice, using nuclei from ovary cells, and bred the mice for three generations. Since then, numerous mammals have been cloned, including monkeys. Currently there is a strong injunction against the cloning of human beings. Federal funds cannot be used to carry a cloned embryo to term, and private laboratories are under severe pressure not to do so. In February 2004, Korean scientist Hwang Woo Suk announced that his team had successfully cloned human blastocysts and were able to extract viable stem cells that may be used in disease treatment. The scientist stressed, however, that he was against reproductive cloning of humans. Nevertheless, under government sanction or not, someone out there will one day successfully clone a human. And when that occurs, a multitude of questions about the consequences of the event will be asked.

Questions for Discussion

- How will society change under conditions of reproduction by cloning?

- What can happen to the structure of the family?

- What value will sexual reproduction have in the face of the certainties of asexual reproduction?

- Will cloning lead to the loss of diversity, a tendency for homogeneity?

- How can society accommodate a population of clones destined to serve the needs of the few?

- How would the society reorganize itself to include clones of the brilliant, the talented in entertainment, the political leaders, the scientists, and the technicians?

For Further Reading

Burbel, P. August 18, 2003. Clone, *World Book Online Reference Center.* Available online at *www.worldbookonline.com.*

Campbell, N. A., J. B. Reece, and L. G. Mitchell. 1999. *Biology.* Menlo Park, CA: Benjamen/Cummings.

Suk Hwang, W., Y. J. Ryu, J. H. Park, E. S. Park, E. G. Lee, J. M. Koo, H. Y. Chun, B. C. Lee, S. K. Kang, S. J. Kim, C. Ahn, J. H. Hwang, K. Y. Park, J. B. Cibelli, and S. Y. Moon. Evidence of a pluripotent human embryonic stem cell line derived from a cloned blastocyst. Published February 12, 2004 online in *Science Express* at *www.sciencemag.org/ scienceexpress/recent.shtml.*

Thompson, B., and B. Harrub. 2001. *Human cloning and stem-cell research—Science's "slippery slope."* Montgomery, AL: Apologetics Press.

Are We Ready for Clones?

As late as 1984, scientists David McGrath and Davor Solter wrote in the journal *Science,* "The cloning of mammals by simple nuclear transfer is biologically impossible." That assertion has been proven false, and since that date sheep, mice, cows, monkeys—a virtual menagerie of mammals—have been cloned. A moratorium on the cloning of humans has been enforced by law and by intimidation. Yet the announcement of the first true human clone— from somatic cell and egg cell fusion to embryonic birth—is only a question of time. Whether it occurs in a federal laboratory or in a private clinic, it will happen.

And when it happens, will society be prepared? Here's a hypothetical example: Let's say Clone #1 is successfully created. The clonal cells were stomach cells of a seven-year-old male. The egg cell with the nucleus removed came from a 35-year-old woman. The male donor has a 205 IQ with an interest in astrophysics. The female donor is also unusual with superior skills in Olympic track and field. The embryo developed and the fetus grew in the uterus of a birth mother for nine months. The birth was normal, the child

was normal, but from the instance of birth, Clone #1 began a most unusual life.

Who was his father? His mother? What is his name? What is his genealogy? Can he reproduce? Who are his children's grandparents?

Let us now see how his life is developing. First, with whom does he spend his life? With his father and mother, or the nearest relatives? Or, does he become a ward of the state? Harder questions lie ahead. Take on the task of writing the biography of this first human clone. Try to anticipate his experiences as the very first human clone, and possibly his adventures with a new kind of life in an uncharted society. What are his experiences with longevity? Genetic memory? Social action? Social interaction? Marriage?

Now if Clone #1 becomes one of a large population of identical clones performing a task for the good of the community, how is he to be integrated into the society? For example, say Clone #1, along with thousands of nearly identical clones, is selected by society to protect Earth from impending hazards from outer space. Do the clones become human shields, putting their lives at risk to save our own? Or are the clones to be treated as human as anyone else? Or will the clones, by reason of their select superior skills, become the chosen few to make the ultimate decisions and lead the way?

Compose your essay of the world with clones—their impact on us and our impact on them. What will their presence be like? Share your thoughts with the class. Here come the clones, with problems or promises for the future.

Cats and Their Impact on Wildlife Populations

Could you be harboring a killer in your home? Is it possible that cute little cat snoozing so angelically on the sofa is one of the major predators of wildlife in the United States? "Not my cat! She gets a belly full of food every day," reason many cat owners. Yet the fact is that even the well-fed cat will prowl night and day, catching and killing small birds and mammals—a death toll that may be contributing to the loss of some rare species. Do you know the devastation to wildlife caused by free-running cats? Cats are genetically programmed to hunt small animals—not because they are hungry, but because the animals are there. The cat's prey is usually batted and mauled to death, but seldom eaten. Perhaps the easiest solution to the problem is to lock the cat up inside the house, and let it be a *house* pet.

In contrast, in rural America, where cats live in the barn, the house, or other structure, they serve an important purpose. Their job is to patrol the farm grounds controlling the vermin. These cats control the pest population, but also attack songbirds and game birds. With a U.S. population of 60 million cats, researchers estimate cats are responsible for the deaths of hundreds of millions of birds each year.

Wisconsin Research Project

Stanley Temple and his graduate student, John Coleman, of the University of Wisconsin at Madison, completed a four-year study of the impact of free-ranging domestic cats on rural wildlife. They monitored about 30 radio-collared cats for various periods of time. They calculated that in Wisconsin alone, cats kill 19 million songbirds and 140,000 game birds in a single year. Cats can be a major threat to bird populations, especially around farms. They estimated that the Western meadowlark population is declining at the annual rate of 8 percent.

One reason cats are doing so much damage is that there are now so many of them. Temple found that 78 percent of the residents in rural Wisconsin had more than four free-roaming cats, giving some counties in that state a density of 57 cats per square mile. (Urban areas record even higher numbers: as many as 1,295 cats per square mile in Madison, Wisconsin.)

The Wisconsin study found that 94 percent of cat owners on farms regretted that cats destroyed songbirds and that 83 percent wanted game birds on their property, yet only 42 percent were willing to reduce the number of cats to reduce the number of birds lost. Cat owners seem to have a lot of denial about the hunting achievement of their cat. In fact, they seem to take certain pride in their kitty's prowess and ability to kill wildlife. The cat came into association with humans long before it became a pet and companion. Originally, cats served as a means to destroy vermin, and only after that did the cat take over the household. The reason there are so many cats on farms is that this is the role they still play, patrolling the barns and fields of the farmer.

The fact that cats hunt has nothing to do with whether they ate or not. Cats hunt for the sake of hunting. In the Wisconsin study, 82 percent of the cats were fed daily by their owners. Why cats bring their trophies home to their masters and mistresses is another mystery, the world over. Famed zoologist Desmond Morris thinks it is because cats think their owner a hopeless hunter. "House cats often treat their human as pseudo parents, but when it comes to hunting they treat the owners as kittens. And if the kittens do not know how to catch and eat small birds, then the cat must demonstrate to them," he writes. Temple thinks the wild cats' cache of uneaten prey is leftover food. He thinks the trophies of pet cats come from the urge to store extra food.

Putting a bell on a cat or declawing a cat can have little to no effect on its ability to stalk or to kill prey. When a cat stalks its prey, it moves with a stealth that makes it nearly motionless. The bell doesn't ring. And declawed cats don't stop hunting. Without claws they simply bat down their prey.

The best solution is to confine cats in their homes. Many owners say that they cannot confine a cat—the cat would go crazy. It is not unfair for cats to remain in the house throughout their lives. In such a condition a cat will live an average of 17 years, while a free-roaming cat will live only three–five years. Indoor cats avoid exposure to feline leukemia and rabies. The greatest danger to outdoor cats is automobiles, which kill 1.5 million a year. And who is to say that the pleasures of the cat are more important than the lives of the birds?

A cat curfew was imposed by the Sherbrooke Shire Council in Victoria, Australia, when it was discovered that night-roaming cats were stalking the rare lyrebirds in the nearby forests. The council ruled that all cats must be kept in at night and imposed a $100 fine for violators. The curfew on cats roaming at night saved the lyrebirds.

But on farms the cat must be free to roam, to catch the rats, mice, and other vermin. One solution is to cut down on their population through birth control. An estimated 35,000 kittens are born in the United States each day, compared with 10,000 humans. One female and her offspring can produce 420 cats in just seven years.

The population problem has the wildlife managers scratching their heads. Federal and state wildlife agencies spend a lot of money on incentives for farmers to provide habitat for wildlife, but that might be a waste of money if the environment is overrun with cats.

The Ups and Downs of Cats in History

In 3500 BCE the Egyptian cat looked like the one in your window. It was welcomed into granaries and homes to control the rodents. The cat's eye flashed in the night, giving the Egyptians the notion the cat had special powers for seeing at night. The combination of night vision and the power of reflective light convinced the Egyptians that cats were empowered by the sun god Ra. They deified the cat, and erected temples to the cat goddess Bastet. Laws were enacted to protect the lives of cats. When cats died they were mummified, given funerals and owners shaved their eyebrows.

Later, cats were smuggled out of Egypt and sold in Europe for prize money. The Europeans were able to save so much grain from rodents that Europe's economic recovery was credited to the cat. In 1484 Pope Innocent the Eighth empowered the Inquisition to burn all cats and cat lovers, claiming they were in league with the devil. The result was a reduction in the cat population and a huge increase in the rodent population. This led, in large measure, to the famine and the plague. In America the cat was feared for its alleged supernatural power, but still respected for its pest control.

For Further Reading

Cats and wild birds don't mix. Available online at *www.wildbirds.com/protect_cats.htm*.

Coleman, J. S., and S. A. Temple. 1993. Rural residents' free-ranging domestic cats: A survey. *Wildlife Society Bulletin* 21: 381–90.

Else, R. 1995. House cats: No. 1 small game killer. *Fur-Fish-Game* (April).

Gibbons, W. 2000. Cats need another look. *Ecoviews* (May 7). Available online at *www.uga.edu/srel/ecoviews5-7-00.htm*.

Harrison, G. 1992. Is there a killer in your house? *National Wildlife* (October/ November).

Morris, D. 1986. *Catwatching: Why cats purr and everything else you wanted to know.* New York: Three Rivers Press.

U.S. Fish and Wildlife Service. Migratory songbird conservation pamphlet. T. Ross, ed.

Cats: What's the Dilemma?

Cats are the cause of the loss of between 20 and 140 million birds in Wisconsin alone annually. Similar numbers are true for all states. The simplest cure for the entire country would be for cat owners to confine their cats indoors. The cat would not get out into the natural world where birds, rabbits, mice, and lizards live. The cat would become an obligate indoor animal.

On the other hand, owners of cats that live on farms have an obligation to have the cats serve the farmer not as a pet, but as a working pest controller. The cat serves the farmer's need for pest control in exchange for room and board.

Thus there are two kinds of cats, one that lives in the owner's house and does not leave the premises, and one that lives on the farmer's property and has free range of the land.

1. Will the cat that lives in the house ever tire of memories of the hunt? Will he ever give up or give in to his fate as a hunter? Will her kittens or her kittens' kittens forget the moves and strategies of the hunt?

2. Will the cat that lives on the farm always be a hunter? Suppose he is retired to a city apartment, and spends the rest of his life acting out the hunt for birds while staring out the window. What kind of cat will he become, now denied the hunt?

Photodisc

3 In an experiment, six cats being fed their preferred diet were distracted by little white rats. The cats interrupted their dinner, killed the rats without eating them, and then resumed eating their dinners. What does this say about the relationship between the cats' dining preferences and hunting?

4 Domestic cats are an introduced species of predator and as such compete with foxes, raccoons, and skunks. What might be the fate of these native predators if the cats become established as a more successful predator? What might be the fate of birds and small mammal prey?

5 What sort of laws can be written that would allow farmers to permit their cats to roam free, while city owners would be required to confine their pet cats indoors?

Cat Behavior Survey

No matter where you live, there are probably cats living in the houses, apartments, and farmhouses around you. Conduct a survey. Grab a clipboard, several sheets of paper, and a pen. Start out by practicing on each other for a while.

Name _____

Address _____

Describe the cat population of the neighborhood. _____

_____

Do you have cats? _____ How many? _____ Have you a dog? _____ How many? _____

How long per day are cat(s) free to roam (in and out, out most of time, in most of time, in all time)? _____

What do they do when outside? potty? hunt? look around? wonder? _____

_____

Has your cat ever brought you an animal (bird, rodent) from the hunt? _____

Do cats that stay indoors become avid bird-watchers? _____

Are your cats neutered? _____

Are your cats declawed? _____

What additional behaviors of the cats in your neighborhood have you observed? _____

_____

Stem Cell Transplants

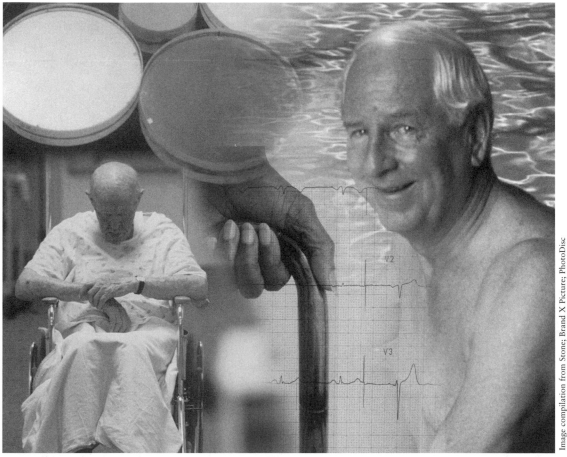

Image compilation from Stone; Brand X Picture; PhotoDisc

Transplanting embryonic stem cells from embryo into adult as a means of rejuvenating diseased cells, tissues, and organs poses ethical and moral challenges. In recent years stem cell–derived nerve and glandular tissue has been transplanted into the brains and pancreas of Parkinson's disease and diabetes patients, respectively, with mixed results. The embryonic stem cells were at first derived from the 1.5 million embryos aborted each year in the United States. But today, the embryonic stem cells mostly come from the surplus of three- to five-day-old blastocysts of women who are stockpiling and freezing embryos for fertility purposes. Those frozen blastocysts that are not used become available to research. Still, there are questions about how the excess embryos in the procedures are to be used or disposed of by the woman and about the involvement of physicians and clinics in marketing the embryonic and transplant techniques. Apparently, the morality of using cells acquired through induced abortion almost ceases to be a major issue since stem cell lines have not been derived from abortions. Nevertheless, the question of the "slippery slope" continues to gnaw at the procedure that begins with the harvesting of cells from a living human.

Background

Stem cell research is furthering knowledge about how an organism develops from a single embryonic cell, and how a healthy cell replaces a damaged cell in an adult organism. Among the practical outcomes of the research is the connection to cell-based therapies to treat diseases in what is called *regenerative medicine*. Yet, stem cell research raises more questions than it answers.

Figure 5

Stem cell cultivation

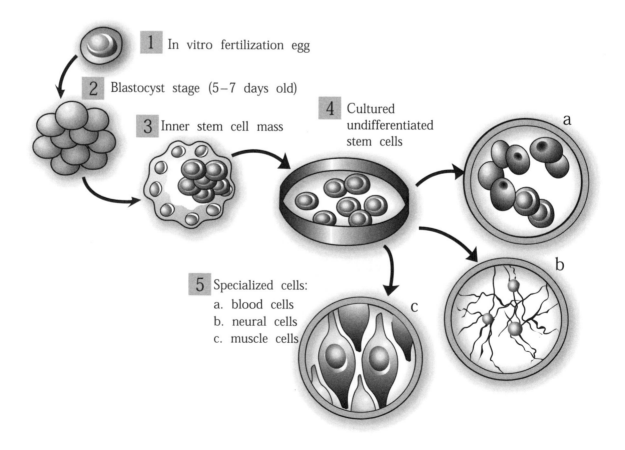

1 In vitro fertilization egg

2 Blastocyst stage (5–7 days old)

3 Inner stem cell mass

4 Cultured undifferentiated stem cells

5 Specialized cells:
   a. blood cells
   b. neural cells
   c. muscle cells

a

b

c

Stem cells have unique characteristics. First, they are unspecialized cells that can reproduce themselves for long periods of time by cell division. Second, under special physiologic and experimental conditions they can be induced to become specialized cells with special functions, such as a secretary neuron in the brain or a beating cell in the heart.

Two major kinds of stem cells occur in the body: the embryonic stem cell and the adult (somatic) stem cell. Embryonic stem cells lie inside the cell mass of the blastocyst. The blastocyst forms about two to five days after fertilization and contains a disc of about 30 cells. The trophoblast is a mass of cells that surrounds the blastocyst; a blastocoel is the hollow cavity inside the embryo. The 30 embryonic stem cells are each pluripotent, and capable of changing into any cell of the body.

The adult (somatic) stem cells migrate with the tissue they form. For a while it was believed that blood stem cells gave rise to blood tissue only, but recently it's been shown they possess plasticity, that is, they can give rise to a number of different cells, such as nerve cells and liver cells.

All stem cells, regardless of origin, have three properties: they are capable of renewing themselves by dividing for long periods of time as a stem directs, they can remain indefinitely unspecialized, and they can give rise to specialized cell types. Embryonic stem cells can become any kind of specialized cell, whereas adult stem cells are generally limited to differentiat-

Stem cells offer the possibility of a renewable source of replacement cells to treat a myriad of diseases, conditions, and disabilities including:

- Parkinson's disease
- Alzheimer's disease
- spinal cord injury
- stroke
- burns
- heart disease
- diabetes
- osteoarthritis and
- rheumatoid arthritis.

Information courtesy of the National Institutes of Health stem cell information page. Available online at *http://stemcells.nih.gov.*

ing into cell types restricted to their tissue of origin, with the recent exception noted above.

Cells in the bodies of developing young mammals gradually change from a stage of nondifferentiation to a stage of irreversible commitment to a specific form and function. For example, undifferentiated cells from the brain of an early embryo do not yet know that they are brain cells. Transplanted into the brain of an adult, they produce tumor-like growths. Brain cells from fetuses older than three months have already differentiated and have started to develop axon and dendrites. By now they have lost the capacity to regenerate parts. Brain cells of the 11-week-old embryo, however, know that they are brain cells, but have not yet differentiated axon and dendrite processes and the synaptic connections of functioning cells. Therefore when transplanted into adult brains, these cells can integrate and mature with the tissues of the brain of an adult host. They stimulate the growth of such supporting tissues as blood vessels. As they mature further they can secrete hormones essential to normal functioning.

Another characteristic of embryonic cells transplanted into adults is their general acceptance by the immune system of the host. When the donor embryonic stem cells are from a species different than the host, however, rejection usually occurs unless suppressor drugs are used.

Stem Cells for the Future Treatment of Parkinson's Disease

Parkinson's disease is a common neurodegenerative disorder that affects more than 2 percent of the population over 65 years of age. Parkinson's disease is caused by a progressive degeneration and loss of dopamine-producing neurons, which leads to tremors, rigidity, and an abnormally decreasing mobility. It is thought that Parkinson's disease may be the first disease to be amenable to treatment using stem cell transplantation. Factors that support this notion include knowledge of the cell type DA (dopamine-producing neurons) needed to relieve the symptoms of the disease. In addition, several laboratories have been successful in developing methods to induce embryonic stem cells to differentiate into cells with many of the functions of DA neurons.

In a recent study, scientists directed mouse embryonic stem cells to differentiate into DA neurons by introducing the gene Nurr 1. When transplanted into the brains of a rat model of Parkinson's disease, these stem cell–derived DA neurons reinnervated the brains of the mouse Parkinson's disease model, released dopamine, and improved motor function.

Regarding human stem cell therapy, scientists are developing a number of strategies for producing dopamine neurons from human stem cells in the laboratory for transplantation into humans with Parkinson's disease. The successful creation of an unlimited supply of dopamine neurons could make neurotransplantation widely available for Parkinson's patients at some time in the future.

Perhaps the application for human stem cells with the most potential is the generation of cells and tissues for the cell-based therapies. The demand for donated organs and tissues far outweighs the supply. Stem cells could possibly be directed toward the production of replacement cells and tissues to treat Parkinson's disease, Alzheimer's disease, spinal cord injury, stroke, burns, heart disease, diabetes, osteoarthritis, and rheumatoid arthritis.

For example it may be possible to develop healthy heart muscle cells in the laboratory and then transplant those cells into patients with chronic heart disease. Preliminary research in mice and other animals indicates that bone marrow stem cells, transplanted into a damaged heart, can generate the heart cells and repopulate the heart tissue.

In people diagnosed with type 1 diabetes, the cells of the pancreas that normally produce insulin are destroyed by the patient's own immune system. New studies indicate that it may be possible to direct the differentiation of cultured embryonic stem cells to form insulin-producing cells in the patient's own pancreas.

Issues

Most anti-abortionists challenge the use of embryonic stem cells in scientific and medical research. They believe that the harvesting of human cells from intentionally aborted embryos is as outrageously immoral as the use of the victims of the holocaust in medical research by

Nazi doctors. These opponents of embryonic stem cell research perceive the acquired living cells of the unborn as poison fruit, and no matter how much good can be derived from their use, nothing can redeem the moral wrong of the induced abortion.

Advocates of embryonic stem cell therapy argue that they are operating under a moral code based on compassion and rationality. They believe that the stem cells of embryos are too valuable to discard, and that to ignore this available resource would itself be an immoral act. In the United States alone, medical research with embryonic stem cells offers hope for 2 million diabetics, 1.5 million Parkinson's disease patients and 300,000 persons with spinal injuries. Against the argument of complicity in abortion, advocates of embryonic stem cell research argue that using these cells no more implicates one in the abortion than using the surviving organs from an automobile accident victim implicates one in the accident.

Beyond the issue of morality of abortion, ethicists have been concerned about how society will regulate an industry based on the use of stem cells, whatever their source. One projection envisages a $6 billion per-year medical business: As stem cell transplants become routine, some fear the market of stem cells will take control of physicians and clinics. Or, women may be persuaded to become pregnant, schedule their abortions, and designate the person who is to receive their stem cells—or even sell their stem cells in a personal business.

In 2001, President George W. Bush created the Presidential Council on Bioethics and appointed Leon Kass, a respected bioethicist, as chair. The task was to recommend action on cloning and stem cell research. In July 2002 the committee gave the president a report in which the majority of the council recommended a temporary ban on all human cloning research. But on a closely related issue—the continuation of embryonic stem cell research—a temporary ban on the funding of all new stem cell lines remains in force. Government funding for cloning has halted, and only a trickle of preexisting stem cell lines are available for government use.

Questions for Discussion

You may find the questions on the accompanying student page sufficient to provoke discussions of which direction stem cell research and treatment should take. The following questions could stimulate deeper thinking on this issue:

- Someone observed that transplanting parts of the dead (embryos and adult organs) to parts of the living is one of the strangest things humans have ever done. Will the security of being the person you were born as be affected by sharing your body with functional cells of an unborn embryo or the heart of another adult?

- When the National Institutes of Health suspended funding to 116 embryonic stem cell research projects, researchers protested the action was dangerous to American interests. They argued that if the U.S. government didn't support this research, private companies and foreign governments would go forward without the safeguards NIH regulations ensure. How valid are such protests about money, regulation, and competition?

- A young woman's father has Alzheimer's disease. She is seeking help in becoming pregnant with her father's sperm so she can grow the most genetically compatible stem cells for transplant. Should she and participating specialists be permitted to pursue this project?

■ How are full organ transplants and embryonic stem cell transplants similar to and different from each other? Could embryonic stem cells of a healthy heart muscle be grown in a culture of a diseased heart and then be transplanted directly into a diseased heart?

For Further Reading

Chapman, A. R. et al. Stem cell research and applications: Monitoring the frontiers of biomedical research. *The AAAS/ISC report on stem cell research.* Available online at *www.counterbalance.net/stemcell/index-frame.html.*

Embryonic stem cell research at the University of Wisconsin-Madison. Available online at *www.news.wisc.edu/packages/stemcells/index.html?get=facts.*

National Institutes of Health. Stem cell information. Available online at *http://stemcells.nih.gov/infoCenter/stemCell Basics.asp.*

Should Embryonic Stem Cell Research and Transplants be Permitted?

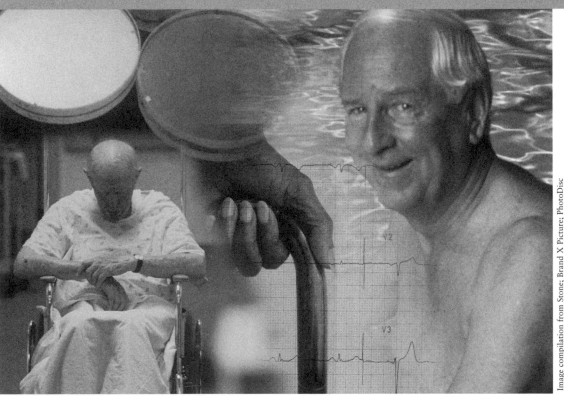

Image compilation from Stone; Brand X Picture; PhotoDisc

Someday soon the living stem cells of embryos may keep adults alive, healthy, and youthful. Stem cells at the proper stage of development can mature and function normally if transplanted into the organs of mature humans.

People with such degenerative disorders as Parkinson's disease, paralysis, and insulin-dependent diabetes could replace their degenerative cells with new healthy cells by means of an embryonic stem cell operation. While the procedure is still in experimental stages, early results with humans appear to be promising. As research and medical applications of stem cell transport go forward, philosophers have already started delving into the ethical issues involved in putting the living stem cells from aborted embryos, or from adult stem cells, into the bodies of people for whom new tissue means longer, happier lives.

Today, the use of embryonic stem cells for any purpose arouses strong emotional responses, because of its relation to the grave moral issues associated with abortion, and the status of human embryos and fetuses. The questions that follow have provoked a considerable amount of controversy.

Questions to Consider

1 Under what circumstances would you accept the stem cell of an aborted embryo to cure you of diabetes or a parent of Parkinson's disease?

2 Suppose the numbers of induced abortions in the United States declined dramatically due to the passage of anti-abortion legislation or the increased and effective use of birth control procedures. How might the stem cell industry meet its demand for human embryos? Should we buy and import embryos from countries where induced abortion is legal?

3 What limits, if any, should be imposed on embryonic stem cell transplant research and development? Should stem cells be injected into the facial skin of the aged who want to appear young with a rejuvenated face? Will the replacement of degenerated tissues and organs extend the human life span beyond the best interests of our species?

4 Would the medical use of embryonic stem cells have brutalizing effects on our society that would outweigh the good of medical progress? Would our reverence for life erode a little more each time an unborn human embryo is used to extend the life and attractiveness of an adult?

Chemical and Biological Weapons of Mass Destruction

The Iraq war of 2003 was reported to be about chemical and biological weapons of mass destruction. The United States and England claimed Iraq possessed large stores of chemical and biological weaponry that it was prepared to use against its enemies. The Iraqi government denied the accusation but was not fully cooperative with inspectors who were looking for weapons. The United States and England invaded Iraq. Of course, there were other reasons for the conflict, but the alleged possession of weapons of mass destruction was the stated cause of the hostilities. One year after the invasion, no weapons had been found. Does this mean there were none? Or, were the weapons destroyed? Or, are the weapons hidden somewhere?

During World War I, when the combatants exchanged poison gas on the battlefield and killed and maimed thousands of soldiers and civilians, most people in the world became horrified by the complicity of it all. The majority of the people could not abide a military that would poison every man, woman, and child of the enemy. Nevertheless, the United States

PhotoDisk

maintains an up-to-date chemical and biological weapons program designed to deter enemies.

Chemical Warfare

Chemical warfare began in prehistoric times with the use of such weapons as poisoned arrows. Later, during the siege of Athens in about 400 BC, the Athenians were attacked by the Spartans with irritating sulfur dioxide, produced by burning sulfur with pitch upwind of the city.

World War I was the beginning of modern-day chemical warfare. In 1914 the French lobbed the first tear gas grenades; the Germans retaliated with tear gas in artillery shells. On April 22 of the following year, the Germans used chlorine gas in Belgium, killing about 5,000 Allied soldiers. The Germans released the first mustard gas, $S(CH_2CH_2CL)_2$, and phosgene, $COCl_2$, against the Allies in 1917 at Verdun. By the end of World War I, about 3,000 different toxic chemicals had been considered for use in war. Millions were killed by these substances.

The 1925 Geneva protocols outlawed the first-strike use of chemical and biological warfare. (The United States ratified this treaty in 1974.) Even so, since the Geneva protocols, gas has been used by Italians against Ethiopians, Japanese against Chinese, Egyptians against Yemenites, and Iraqis against Iranians. Although no gases are known to have been used in World War II, the Germans did test nerve gases on concentration camp prisoners.

During the Vietnam War, the United States used nonlethal riot control gas in tactical situations, claiming that these harassing types of agents do not qualify as war gases prohibited by the Geneva protocols.

Antipersonnel chemical weapons can be grouped according to their physiological effects. Nerve agents are the most lethal chemi-cal munitions for strategic and tactical warfare. These organophosphorus compounds interfere with the proper transmission of nerve impulses, by irreversibly inhibiting acetylcholinesterase, an enzyme crucial to the operation of the nervous system.

There are two classes of nerve gases—the earlier, less toxic G agents and the modern, highly toxic V agents. The first of the G agents was GA, with the name tabun and the formula shown in Figure 6. Of the toxic V agents, agent VX is probably the most deadly, because of the small dosage required to kill. But there is no reason to believe that the limit of lethality of nerve gas has been reached.

Chemical agents of lower lethality than nerve gases include blistering agents, choking agents, and blood agents. This category includes the blistering agent mustard gas and the choking agent phosgene. As a blood agent, hydrogen cyanide affects the absorption of oxygen by hemoglobin. These chemicals can cause great pain and, often, lingering death.

Of lowest lethality are the riot control agents and the relatively new incapacitating agents. Riot control agents can cause such reactions as tearing, sneezing, itching, and vomiting. Chloroacetophenone is the tear gas known as Mace (Figure 7). Adamsite is the vomit gas diphenylaminochloroarsine (Figure 8). The dosage of these agents required to disperse rioters is much less than lethal levels, but even small doses can be lethal to victims in confined spaces or who are young, sick, or old.

H. G. Wells introduced the concept of incapacitating agents in *Things to Come* (1935), a fictional story of two warring nations locked in a hopeless suicidal conflict. The story's protagonist gasses the weary warriors on both sides with an anesthetic that induces narcosis long enough

FIGURE 6

GA

Tabun

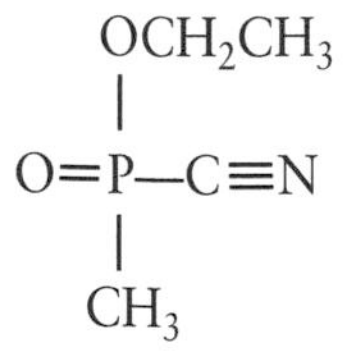

$$OCH_2CH_3$$
$$O=P-C\equiv N$$
$$CH_3$$

FIGURE 7

chloroacetophenone

Mace
(Tear Gas)

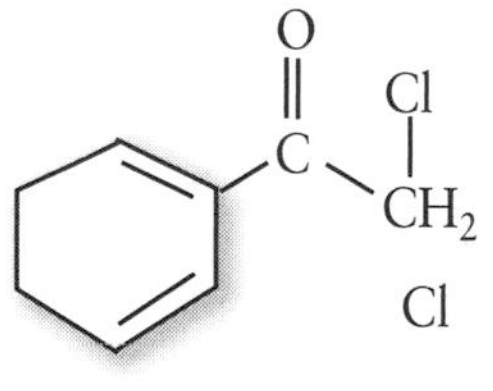

FIGURE 8

diphenylaminochloroarsine

Adamsite
(Vomit gas)

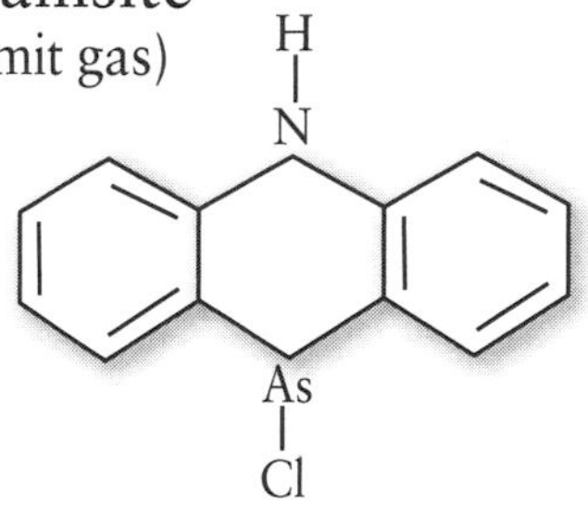

for disarmament. Physical incapacitating agents are attractive nonlethal weapons, because as proposed by H. G. Wells, they promise humane warfare with neither pain nor death. They physically immobilize people by inducing sleep, paralyzing skeletal muscles, or making it impossible to remain standing without fainting.

Military expenditures for chemical weapons are high, with more than 1 billion dollars per year spent in the United States alone. As early as the 1950s, 20 percent of our warfare budget went toward research and development of physically incapacitating agents. At the present time, the United States is believed to possess only one incapacitating agent, BZ. Presumably this agent is a reversible inhibitor of acetylcholinesterase, in contrast to lethal nerve gas, which is an irreversible inhibitor. Research strategies and combat findings have been and still are top military secrets, so the practicality of bloodless combat with incapacitating agents is unknown.

One of the most serious problems with using physically incapacitating agents as strategic weapons is that their dosage may range into lethality for the general population. That is, the quantities of gases dropped on civilian targets can be adjusted for normal adults, but such doses can be fatal to children, the elderly, or the sick. The problem is compounded because weapons sprayed into the air cannot be aimed and fired like bullets—gases and smokes drift with the changing winds.

Testing incapacitating agents presents another dilemma. Researchers cannot assess the usefulness of a chemical agent without testing on human subjects. Chemicals that only incapacitate test animals such as rabbits, goats, and monkeys might have different effects on human test subjects, perhaps severely injuring or killing them. So, who could ethically be tested?

Biological Warfare

Biological warfare research got underway in 1941, as researchers began studying defensive measures rather than offensive activities. In the beginning, the scientists were interested in studying measures that would treat diseases with vaccination and medication, rather than weaponizing the bacteria and viruses. In January 1943, a researcher at Cornell University began studying botulism as a weapon, and a team at Harvard Medical School sought to study anthrax. Both agents are deadly forms of diseases and remained the foci of biological research for the duration of World War II. From then on, the policy makers in Washington determined the nature of the weapons program, and not the biologists in the laboratories. In late 1943, with technical assistance from the British, the Americans started making 500-pound anthrax bombs, with 104 4-pound bombs inside each that would scatter and shatter upon impact. The bombs were not tested, however, though it was known that pulmonary anthrax was nearly always fatal. Before the factory could complete the bombs, the war with Germany ended. Also during the war, the Germans were thought to be considering using their V-l "buzz bombs" to drop biological weapons on England. Without enough biological weapons, the best the Allies could do was retaliate with poison gas. Fortunately, it was a standoff, with neither the Allies nor the Germans resorting to chemical or biological weapons.

In late 1944, George Merck sent a report to Secretary of State Cordell Hunt and General George Marshall stating that his team was investigating four new "agents against men." These were brucellosis (undulant fever), psittacosis (parrot fever), tularemia (rabbit fever), and respiratory glanders (a contagious disease of horses and mules). The American experience during wartime warns that weapons designed for deterrence or retaliation may become attractive and seem morally justifiable for offensive strikes. It may not be easy for people to constrain the use of a technology they have created to settle a just war.

Questions for Discussion

You may find the accompanying student pages sufficient to provoke discussion about the wisdom of using nonlethal physically incapacitating agents in war and in police work. The following questions could stimulate deeper thinking on the issue.

■ The Germans discovered and produced nerve gas in the 1930s. They tested it and used it on prisoners in concentration camps. However, they never used it against the Soviets or the British, even when their victory was threatened. Why do you think they did not use their nerve gas against their enemies?

■ Soldiers were ordered to attend the testing of nuclear weapons in the 1950s. Do you think the military should have the right to ask a soldier to participate in the testing of incapacitating agents? Do you think prison inmates should be offered reductions in sentences, or commutation of death sentences, in exchange for participation in tests of incapacitating agents? Why do you think so?

■ Suppose that during World War II either Japan or the United States (but not both) had highly effective nonlethal incapacitating agents. How might the war have been different?

■ How is it that all nations must be prepared for biological warfare, yet no nation expects to be touched by it? But if one nation does not have protection from biological warfare, does that nation stand vulnerable to a holocaust?

■ A person who works in the "hot room" of a biological laboratory is inoculated for the diseases to which he or she may be exposed. Why doesn't the government inoculate all citizens against "hot" diseases?

For Further Reading

Bernstein, B. J. 1987. The birth of the U.S. biological-warfare program. *Scientific American* 25 (6): 116–21.

Hersh, S. 1968. *Chemical and biological warfare.* Indianapolis: Bobbs-Merrill Company.

Stockholm International Peace Research Institute. 1971. *The problem of chemical and biological warfare,* 6 vols. New York: Humanities Press.

Young, J. A. T., and R. J. Collier. 2002. Attaching anthrax. *Scientific American* 286 (3): 48–59.

Can New Incapacitating Weapons Lead to Humane Warfare?

Getty Images

Nearly all modern warfare is chemical. Most weapons depend on chemical reactions to burn and blast. But society usually uses the term *chemical warfare* to refer to the intentional exposure of people to toxic substances that can kill, sicken, or incapacitate.

Thousands of different compounds have been developed and tested for their toxicity. The most deadly of all is the nerve gas VX. A drop of VX the size of the period at the end of this sentence is fatal. Nerve gas kills people the same way Raid kills roaches, by blocking the proper transmission of nerve impulses, resulting in paralysis and death.

Blistering and choking gases, such as mustard gas and phosgene, are less deadly than nerve gases, but cause severe irritation of skin, eyes, and lungs. In war, each victim of these agents requires help from several other soldiers. The chaos resulting from mustard gas or phosgene attacks might shorten a war… or invite retaliation.

In recent years, chemical warfare researchers have been developing two categories of nonlethal chemical agents that incapacitate people. "Off the rocker" agents such as LSD-25 can neutralize a population by making victims incapable of realizing what they are doing for hours. Military strategists have nearly abandoned these psychologically incapacitating agents out of fear that mass madness might panic bewildered leaders into nuclear war.

"On the floor" agents cause people to collapse by lowering their blood pressure, putting them to sleep, or blocking the operation of their involuntary muscles. A highly secret chemical, known as BZ, may act on the nervous system in a way similar to nerve gas. BZ is thought to be a true "on the floor" incapacitant, as opposed to disabling chemicals such as Mace. Mace is a highly purified form of tear gas, a riot control agent. It severely irritates nerve endings in eyes and mucus membranes, making those sprayed with it very uncomfortable. But, while Mace is a nonlethal chemical agent, it is not a true incapacitating agent.

Question to Consider

1 Do you think our military should be conducting research to develop nonlethal physically-incapacitating agents? Why do you think as you do?

2 Assume that decades of high-priority research have produced incapacitating agents that can immobilize people as effectively as nerve gas can kill them. Under what conditions should these incapacitating agents be used? Should they be used strategically (against an enemy's ability to make war)? Tactically (on the battlefield)? Against terrorists? Against rioting prison inmates? In a hijacked plane on the ground?

3 How do you think nations will react to the first use of incapacitating agents?

4 Develop a scenario describing an ethical response to an enemy chemical or biological attack.

5 Given the development of nonlethal agents, can you think of any circumstances in which lethal chemicals should be used?

Robotic Versus Manned Space Travel

BrandXPictures

I s it time to rethink the manned space program? Despite the Columbia, Challenger, and Apollo disasters, NASA has called for the shuttle program to continue. President Bush's January 2004 initiative for a moon base and manned flights to Mars has led to much discussion about cost, safety, and priorities.

What have the past Apollo adventure projects provided beyond adventure? Scientists have skillfully studied weightlessness. Extensive space sickness studies have been carried out to keep the crew healthy. Yet, what benefits have come to the 6 billion people of the world on the ground? After 40 years, is it time to examine the hard results?

BrandXPictures

...unmanned satellites benefit everyone on Earth. One can turn on a television, make a long distance call, or hook into the Internet.

In contrast, unmanned satellites benefit everyone on Earth. One can turn on a television, make a long distance call, or hook into the Internet. Weather satellites provide minute-to-minute accurate information, and monitoring ground motion around the Earth can predict earthquakes, fault shifts, and volcano eruptions. Earth-orbiting satellites have revolutionized astronomy. Just consider the Hubble telescope scanning the heavens from space since 1990 and sending to Earth the fabulous photographs of the universe's beginning.

Manned space flight in Earth orbit is inefficient, and somewhat dangerous, but not overwhelmingly expensive. Mars space flight is another story. The cost of getting people there and back would be one trillion dollars! Biology is the reason to go there. If we were to find a live bacterium in the sedimentary rock of Mars, that would be a monumental discovery. But humans are loaded inside and outside with bacteria that would surely contaminate the Martian environment and defeat the scientific purpose of the mission. Furthermore, the remote-controlled Mars rovers have successfully discovered tan-

talizing hints of water on Mars without the expense or risk of human travel.

Recently the U.S. Air Force began to use long-range missiles and drones. These missiles can be fired from a great distance with precision and accuracy, and drone planes flown with great speed and maneuverability without a pilot are already operational. Neither the missile nor the drone endangers its pilots, who sit far removed from the action. The missile is guided, and the drone pilot sits at a "desk" with a joystick. In the "old days" the pilots often did not return, or were rescued at great danger and expense by helicopter. The drone planes are much less expensive and far more expendable than any current fighter plane.

Perhaps the parallel between the Air Force, with its piloted planes and its missiles and drones, and NASA, with its manned and unmanned space ships, is not fully comparable. Nevertheless they have these features in common: Unmanned drones and unmanned spacecraft are much cheaper to build; they require none of the accouterments for supporting a living crew; they are lighter; and they are not limited by the physi-

NATIONAL SCIENCE TEACHERS ASSOCIATION

Manned space flight in Earth orbit is inefficient, and somewhat dangerous, but not overwhelmingly expensive. Mars space flight is another story. The cost of getting people there and back would be one trillion dollars!

BrandXPictures

ological limits of a pilot. Furthermore, the unmanned space vehicle does not need to be returned to the Earth—its recorded data can be sent back, and it can go on to eternity.

The $260 million Pathfinder and the Mars rovers are sending streams of data from the Martian surface back to Earth. Meanwhile, the International Space Station has been bedeviled by a seemingly endless stream of accidents. The Mir space station, brought back to Earth and crashed into the ocean after 15 years in 2001, had several incidents where lives were at great risk, including a fire and a collision with a docking ship. The greatest measurable achievements in space have been made by the unmanned robotic vehicles and instruments.

On the other hand, the greatest exhilaration from space travel has been the manned space adventures. There is nothing like sending men and women into space—the new frontier—at great costs of money, at great personal risk, carrying the stars and stripes, in man-made rigs, into Earth orbit and then off to the Moon, to Mars, and on into space where no other person has dared to tread. Is space travel the ultimate adventure for the dreamer? There is a spiritual importance of manned space flights to the nations of the world. Manned space flight is a confirmation of our destiny to explore, a celebration of us. The world would be a lesser place if it had no ballets and symphonies; would it be a still lesser place if it had no manned space exploration?

Questions for Discussion

■ Are human beings naturally compelled to explore the unknown space beyond our planet?

■ Should unmanned spacecrafts, at a fraction of the cost and no risk of life, carry out exploration?

■ Can humans package the senses of sight, sound, taste, touch, and smell in instruments that can sail off for a few hundred million miles and send back data and pictures that tell more about remote space than any person can gather alone?

For Further Reading

Connolly, M. 1997. We don't give ticker tape parades for robots: Humanity and the lure of space travel. *Cornell Science and Technology Magazine* Summer. Available online at *www.rso.cornell.edu/scitech/archive/97sum/man.html*.

Etzioni, A. To NASA: Bring in the drones. *Christian Science Monitor*, Feb. 11, 2003.

Nelan, T. Is expensive manned space flight worth it? No free lunch at NASA. *ABCNEWS.com*. Available online at *http://more.abcnews.go.com/sections/scitech/marsorbust/mars_unmanned.html*.

President's Commission on Moon, Mars, and Beyond. Available online at *www.moontomars.org*.

Sleep, N. Feb. 4, 2003. Re-thinking NASA's manned space program. *Stanford University News Service*. Available online at *http://www.stanford.edu/dept/news/pr/03/sleepvantage25.html*.

Space Exploration: Man or Machine?

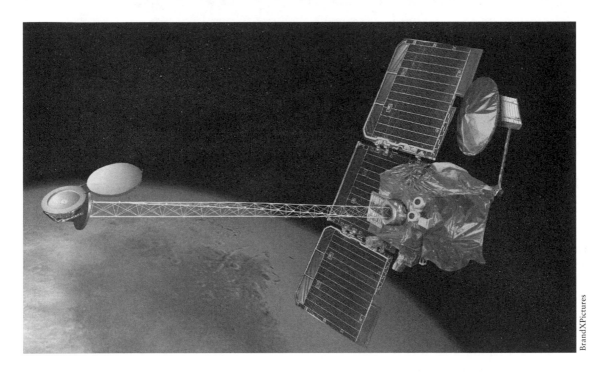

BrandXPictures

Manned space flights are much more expensive than unmanned flights. A flight by a manned space ship to Mars would cost a trillion dollars. The Apollo project to the moon cost 117 billion dollars, and a single shuttle flight into Earth orbit costs $473 hundred million. In contrast, a flight to Mars by Pathfinder was $262 million, Galileo cost $1.4 billion, and voyager was $350 million. The risks of manned space flight are tremendous in lives. In unmanned space flights risks are marginal. Manned space flights yield too little useful information compared with what instruments reveal to us by telemetry. A manned flight must return, while robotic flights can go on and on. Manned flights are strongly influenced by the race for glory, sending the stars and stripes on an adventure into space...and the publicity increases when the astronauts run into trouble. Robotic flights are free of the sense of loss.

Manned space flights are supported by the notion that humans need to explore—in specially protected spacecrafts—but still at great risk to life. And in a sense Congress wants manned space travel to support an industry that builds the costly crafts. Unmanned spacecrafts are supported by scientists who believe that robots, at this stage of space travel, can do anything better than a human can do in space, and send back data at least as well as can humans.

In the end, there seems to be a need to establish a defensible policy that provides a balance between manned and unmanned space travel. Here are some questions for you to think about and discuss.

1   What kinds of information can be gathered by instruments that extend the senses of the human body beyond the capacity of the senses of sight, sound, touch, smell, and taste?

2   How and where on Earth is remote information gathered, recorded, and transmitted by instruments in manners similar to those used on spacecrafts?

3   What kind of information can be obtained by a Sun-orbiting satellite, but not by an instrument located on Earth?

4   Why should people bother to journey into space when there are already instruments that can record data more effectively and efficiently?

5   If a camera on a satellite that circumnavigates the moons of Jupiter takes better pictures at a lesser cost than a manned space vehicle, why should a photographer go?

6   Select one of the unmanned space projects, such as Voyager or Galileo. Find out what data were sought by the unmanned probes or satellites; what sensors were used; how the data were transmitted and recorded; what answers were obtained; and what new questions were then asked.

7   Identify a relatively inaccessible place on Earth such as the bottom of an oil well, the center of an active volcano, or a ventricle of a heart of a chicken. Describe how one would proceed to develop instruments to enter the space and answer questions you would ask.

8   Now identify an equally inaccessible place on the surface of the planet Mars. Drive your space cart and probe into the deep rock, detonate an explosion, read the soundings. Imagine doing this as an astronaut. Imagine doing this as a robot on Earth. Which one was most fulfilling? Why?

9   What evidence shows that humans are naturally compelled to explore the unknown?

10   What are the pro and con arguments for humans to hang up their dream of space adventure, at least until issues of safety, expense of travel, and scientific value of travel are better assured?

11   Why don't we give ticker tape parades for the men and women who invent the space-exploring robots?

12   Compare the perils people face in exploring ocean depths with the hazards of space exploration.

Genetic Screening

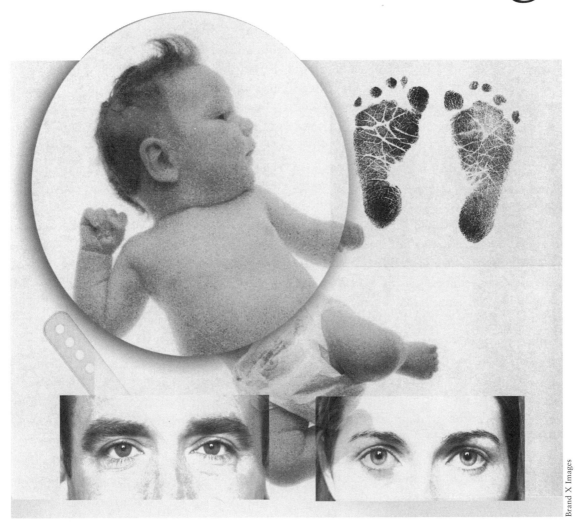

Brand X Images

Many genetic disorders can be detected with tests of blood and chromosomes. Genetic screening is the large-scale use of these tests as part of the public health program. By 1909, physician Archibald Garrod had provided the biochemical knowledge that ultimately led to the screening of newborns.

Garrod's pioneering work helped to establish that alkaptonuria and other metabolic diseases were due to the lack of certain enzymes necessary to catalyze the breakdown of amino acids, which then accumulated in the patients. Garrod also proposed that such disorders could be inherited as Mendelian recessive traits.

PKU, a similar "inborn error of metabolism," was clearly identified by Asbjorn Fölling in 1934. Diagnostic tests for PKU have been available since 1934, but early versions were time-consuming and costly. In 1962 Dr. Robert Guthrie developed a faster, cheaper automated testing procedure for PKU, a disorder that, left untreated, leads to mental retardation and early death. The possibility of identifying PKU children and treating them with a preventative diet led Massachusetts to pass the first *mandatory* PKU screening law in 1963. By 1967, 41 states had passed similar laws.

Genetic screening had reached a new stage in late 1960 when public health officials initiated *voluntary* screening of adults to detect heterozygous carriers of specific recessive traits, such as Tay-Sachs, another degenerative disease. Subsequently, several states passed laws to establish *mandatory* programs to screen for carriers of sickle-cell anemia.

The question of whether genetic screening should be voluntary or mandatory is controversial. So is the goal of the screening—whether to detect *afflicted individuals* or *carriers*. Screening can be performed at various life stages, such as prenatal, neonatal, newborn, or premarital.

Different members of society, worldwide, have advocated genetic screening to achieve different goals. Preventative, or negative, eugenics aims at reducing the frequency of "undesirable" traits in human populations by sterilizing "unfit" individuals or aborting "unfit" fetuses. Genetic screening is more commonly used to provide individuals with information and genetic counseling needed to make decisions about having children, aborting fetuses, and getting timely treatment for afflicted newborns.

Most states recognize their obligation to provide some genetic screening for newborns, especially for such defects as PKU and hypothyroidism, which respond well to therapy. These programs are easy to carry out and are acceptable to the public. But the expansion of genetic screening to cover all newborns and a larger pool of adults for a range of treatable genetic diseases raises a number of issues.

We need to calculate the economic costs and benefits of comprehensive screening of newborns. We must also consider the potential consequences—such as emotional ones—of genetic disease on the family and society; the potential loss of privacy to tested individuals; and the use and abuse of the information by schools, employers, insurance companies, and other private or governmental agencies.

Questions for Discussion

The questions on the accompanying student pages may be sufficient to provoke discussions about genetic screening. The following questions could stimulate deeper thinking on the issue.

- Genetic screening is not foolproof. Some tests can only show the probability that a person is a carrier. Does this weakness affect your thinking on genetic screening? How?

- Premarital screening is practiced to determine the probability of a couple producing children with serious genetic conditions that can deprive the couple of a happy marriage by producing a hopelessly impaired child. Should a couple so informed not get married, marry but not have children, or conceive a child, but test the child *in utero* and abort if the child would have a serious genetic disease?

Brand X Images

- Will mandatory genetic screening programs lead to laws that govern a person's reproductive behavior?

- Whose rights could be violated if genetic screening were mandatory?

- Should members of high-risk ethnic groups be screened selectively—for example, Ashkenazi Jews for Tay-Sachs disease, African Americans for sickle-cell anemia, Scandinavians for PKU, Italians and Greeks for thalassemia?

- Some minority ethnic groups regard genetic screening, which seeks out individuals who should not reproduce, as a thinly veiled genocidal program of majority ethnic groups. What do you think?

For Further Reading

Bhatt, Robin J., *An overview of genetic screening and diagnostic tests in health care The Gene Letter.* Vol. 1 (2). September 1996 at *http://www.geneletter.org*

Massimini, K., ed. 2000. *Genetic disorders Sourcebook.* Detroit, MI: Omnigraphics, Inc.

National Human Genome Research Institute (NHGRI) Office of Policy and Public Affairs, Building 31, Room 4B09, 31 Center Drive, MSC 2580, Bethesda, MD 20892-2580 *www.nhgri.nih.gov*

Wynbrandt, J. et al. 2nd ed. 2000. *Encyclopedia of genetic disorders and birth defects.* New York: Facts on File.

Should We Genetically Screen Newborns?

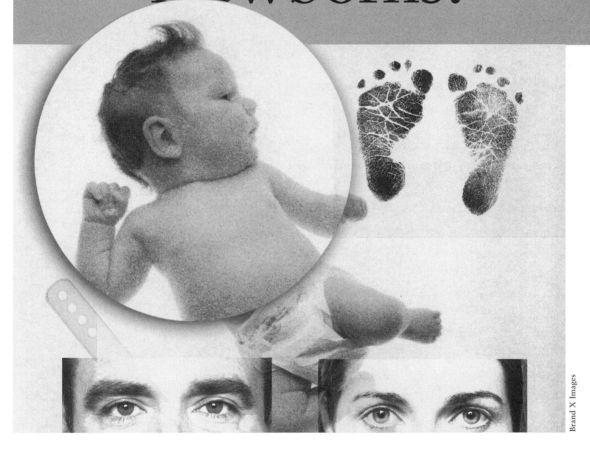

Brand X Images

The genes on our chromosomes play a major role in making us the way we are. *Genetic screening* is the testing of people for particular genes, especially those genes that may cause diseases. More than 3,000 human disorders involve genetic factors.

Screening can be carried out at anytime in the life cycle. People might be screened before birth, after birth, in school, before marriage, or even before employment. In a few years scientists expect to be able to provide people with total gene screens, complete printouts of the approximate 100,000 genes.

The newborns in a hypothetical maternity nursery were genetically screened by blood and chromosome tests. Today's tests found three potentially serious health problems.

Baby #1 This infant has an underactive thyroid gland (hypothyroidism). Replacement hormone treatment will prevent her from being seriously retarded.

Baby #2 This girl is heterozygous for sickle-cell anemia; that is she is a carrier. If she later has a child with a man who is also a carrier of this genetic condition, there is a 25 percent chance that the child will suffer from the deadly disease.

Baby #3 This boy has a sex-linked chromosomal defect, known as fragile-X, that can cause mental retardation and other symptoms. Doctors are treating fragile-X syndrome children successfully with experimental drugs.

Imagine one of the babies with health problems is yours. What would your reaction be to the results of the screening?

Questions to Consider

1 Do you think genetic screening of newborns should be mandatory or voluntary?

2 Whether screening is mandatory or voluntary, who should have access to information about a person's genetic makeup? The tested individual? Parents? School? Governments? Insurance companies? Employers?

3 Should the state require that children who test positive for hereditary diseases undergo treatment to correct genetic defects?

Suppose you were screened as an infant. The test showed that you had a dominant gene for a fatal disease with delayed onset, such as Huntington's disease. When would you want to know about your condition? Why do you feel this way about personal genetic information?

Violence in the Media

J effrey G. Johnson and colleagues at Columbia University and the New York State Psychiatric Institute completed a study in 2002 in which television viewing and aggressive behavior were assessed over a period of 17 years in a population sample of 707 individuals. They concluded that there was a significant association between time spent watching television during adolescence and early adulthood, and the likelihood of subsequent acts of aggression against others. This association remained significant even after previous behavior, parental education, child neglect, family income, neighborhood violence, and psychiatric disorders were controlled statistically. Experimental and longitudinal studies have provided considerable support that violent television watching is associated with increased aggressive behavior. However, most of these other studies investigated short-term increases in aggressive behavior, and few studies have followed subjects for more than a year.

Taxi-Getty Images. Photographer Ron Chapple

Many think that television and other media are primarily responsible for the aggressiveness of American youth and the youth of Western nations. Yet there is an influential group of naysayers who outright deny that the media has anything to do with aggressive behavior in America. They are considered to be like that intimidating minority who, in other areas, claims that smoking doesn't cause cancer and that guns cannot be implicated in violent behavior. Others think that the government's interference with the media's freedom of expression is a worse problem than the one it would attempt to correct. Who is right?

The ancient Romans had violent spectacles that kept the public distracted, engaged, and entertained. They provided the continued violence needed by the warrior state. Are we less bloodthirsty than the Romans because we serve up virtual rather than live spectacles? In the process of raising the level of fictional violence in America, we have eased the access to fantasy far beyond the Roman dreams. Never before has a nation's mind's eyes been so filled with full color images of violence as we have today.

What does the child's eye see? On American television, the elementary school child can see 8,000 murders and another 100,000 acts of violence. By the time the youth turns 18, he or she will have witnessed 40,000 murders. Does the exposure to all of this have no effect on the child because the child knows it is not real? Or does the child not always distinguish acting from reality?

The distinction between responsible and irresponsible portrayal of violence is the debate over media violence. Whether violence has artistic merit is the problem. Can one be assured that violence is packaged in adult themes that are inaccessible to children?

In summary, research literature over the last three decades has been highly consistent in finding three responses to the effect of violence:

1. Increased aggressiveness toward others due to learning and imitation;

2. Increased callousness to real-life violence to others, labeled the *desensitized effect*; and

3. Increased fearfulness (both long term and short term) about becoming a victim of violence—often referred to as the "mean world syndrome."

Questions for Discussion

■ Between 1997 and 1998 there was a rash of shooting in schools by angry students against students and teachers. What were the circumstances and causes of this flare-up? To what extent was the blame put on the media, which may have incited the students to violence? Or, was the media just a scapegoat? What else could have been a cause?

■ Research studies have shown that we are more likely to imitate people who are attractive, respected, and powerful. The more we identify with the character, the more we are likely to imitate the character. Eastwood, Schwarzenegger, and Stallone represent the good guys, but they often portray vigilante hunters who operate outside the law. Do these films support the stereotype that the police and criminal justice system are incompetent and ineffective? What is the effect on the police department of the depiction of the vigilantes as heroes?

■ We need a far more sophisticated discussion about the link between simulated violence and real violence. With the quality of

acting and special effects making it unclear what is fake and what is real blood, real dismemberment, real pain, suffering, and death, how many viewers fail to see the difference? The rational viewer knows the truth. But children in certain stages of development cannot make clear distinctions. Older children can be helped to know that scenes are only made to look real.

■ If producers cut out the gratuitous violence, leaving the essential violence to stay in the plot, wouldn't the real plot be retained? Or

is the gratuitous violence of the stories essential for the rush that sells the script?

■ When it comes to promoting adoration of guns, Hollywood is just as, or more, effective than gun lobbyists in Washington. Has the Hollywood glamorization of guns guided the way for the United States to have more guns on the street than any other nation?

■ Believe it or not, cartoons show the highest levels of violent actions (most acts of violence per program). Doesn't this mean that children's comic commercial cartoons have the highest rate of egregious violence of any media presentation? Is this not a barbaric way to turn the behavior of children from constructive to destructive intent?

For Further Reading

Hepburn, M. A. 2001. Violence in audio-visual media: How educators can respond. *ERIC/ChESS Digest* (April). Available online at *www.indiana.edu/~ssdc/violdig.htm*.

Johnson, J. G. et al. March 29, 2002. Television viewing and aggressive behavior during adolescence and adulthood. *Science.* 295, 2468-71.

Levine, M. 1996. *Viewing violence.* New York: Doubleday.

Newton, D. E. 1996. *Violence and the media.* Santa Barbara, CA: ABC-CLIO, Inc.

Torr, J. D. 2001. *Violence in the media.* San Diego, CA: Greenhaven Press, Inc.

Violence on Television: How Much Is Too Much?

Taxi-Getty Images. Photographer Ron Chapple

In the past 20 years there have been numerous studies and warnings about violent television and movies rousing impressionable youth to violence. Of course there are other factors that can incite violence, such as brutality in home life, exposure to violence in the neighborhood, and easy access to guns. Nevertheless, researchers have pointed to the excessive violence watched on television as a cause of violent behavior among susceptible youth.

Nearly 100 percent of households have TV sets, 87 percent have two or more sets, 60 percent of 12 to 17 year olds have a set in their bedrooms, and cable TV is present in 77 percent of homes. Within households, total TV watching was 59 hours per week in 1998. In addition to standard TV, there is a rising use of TV games, computers, and Internet connections.

Study after study shows that violence occurs in about 57 percent of all programs, with children's TV leading the list. Violence was depicted as humorous in more than a third, and only 4 percent of the programs offered a strong anti-violence message.

While a young viewer of prime-time TV may view three to five violent acts in an hour, Saturday morning TV for children may televise 20 to 25 acts of violence in an hour. TV violence may be especially damaging to children under eight because they cannot tell the difference between the real-life violence and fantasy violence.

The negative effects of viewing violence includes making young people comfortable with violence, possibly rousing them to aggressive behavior, and making children fearful that they will be subject to violence.

Activities

- Review the First Amendment right of freedom of speech that permits creators of TV to write and produce shows containing acts of violence. Set up a debate that argues for and against the position that gratuitous violence on TV pitched to children should be forbidden.

- Examine the rationale for using v-chip technology, the television program rating system, and the feasibility of parental review and application of v-chip technology. What rights do parents have to protect their children from TV that incites them to acts of violence?

- What kind of consumer education for home media consumption can be provided and used by parents?

- One mantra from media executives is to leave parenting decisions to parents. Yet at-risk young people are often the victims of inadequate, ineffective, or even abusive parenting. Does society have a role to play in protecting children from violent material in the media?

- What lessons can be derived from our experiences with banning cigarette advertising, to crush the practice of pitching cigarette smoking to children?

Managed Retreat

PhotoDisc

Around the world, coastlines are retreating. Economic and environmental realities offer two choices: plan a managed retreat now, or undertake a vastly more expensive program of armoring the coastline as required and retreat through a series of unpredictable disasters. This was the prediction of the 1985 Skidway Conference on America's Eroding Shoreline, which proved to be accurate, with the exception that beach nourishment replaced armoring the coast as the method preferred by engineers for stabilizing coastlines. Since that conference, the Atlantic and Gulf coastlines took a beating from such hurricanes as Hugo: 1989, Andrew: 1992, Opal: 1995, George: 1998, and Isabel: 2003.

Their impact caused random retreat at individual property levels and forced communities to reexamine their coastal zone strategies. Although the greenhouse effect is a subject of debate, sea level is rising around the world for most coastlines, and the rate of rise is increasing.

At the close of the 20th century, the Heinz Center for Science, Economics and Environment reported that 10,000 coastal structures in the United States were within the estimated 10-year erosion zone. As of 2000, the coastal counties had a total flood insurance coverage of $466,874,000,000. The best option for many of these properties and their communities is managed retreat. Although retreat has a negative sound for some, the elements of strategic retreat are being incorporated into coastal zone management.

Shift from Engineering to "Soft" Solutions

Historically the method of choice to protect the shoreline has been to use engineering, armoring the beaches against the wind and water of the angry sea. The methods of armoring were to build parallel seawalls, bulkheads, revetments, and offshore breakwaters. Groins and jetties were built perpendicular to the beach.

Then came the replenishment of the beach sand, with quantities added to replace the eroded sand. Or, the beach was scraped and bulldozed in order to release compacted sand. The sand dune volume was increased with sand fencing, raising the frontal dune elevation, and plugging dune gaps. Vegetation was planted on the dunes, and marshes were developed on the sound side.

Next came modification of development and infrastructure: retrofit homes, elevate building sites, enforce lower density development, create back roads terminating in dune gaps, and move utilities to service lines into the interior or bury them below erosion level.

With beaches of the world being beset with more and more people building homes on the coasts of the continents, and more devastating storms tearing the homes down, the old methods of armoring the beach against the elements are failing. At first, the breakwaters, bulkheads, revetments, seawalls, and groins broke the force of the waves and protected the shoreline from the pounding surf. But the rising sea levels and the greater ferocity of the storms are adding to the devastation.

As the armor fails, so do the efforts to replenish the beach with sand. The cost of pumping sand in from offshore sites increases as the source of sand steadily diminishes. Holding the sand with planted vegetation on sand dunes and in marshes on the sound side is seldom enough to withstand a hurricane. The cost to replenish sand at Miami Beach, for example, is very high, but revenues from the many people and the hotels that need it pay the cost. For less high profile beaches, the use by a smaller population does not meet the costs of replenishment.

Managed retreat is the term for the application of coastal zone management and mitigation tools designed to move existing and planned development out of the path of eroding coastlines and coastal hazards. The strategy is based on the idea of moving out of harm's way and encourages people to recognize the dynamics of the coastal zone, which should dictate the kind of management employed.

Abandonment

Often, *abandonment* is an unplanned, poststorm retreat-response to storm destruction of buildings, or land loss. Sometimes entire villages are lost to the sea. Twenty-nine villages were swept out to sea on the English Yorkshire coast during storms in the 20th century. Planned abandonment can be incorporated into managed retreat in several ways. Under this plan, buildings are regarded as having a fixed life span. When that life comes to an end and they fall into the sea, no attempt is made to protect them. Reconstruction inland is planned behind the poststorm setback line. Rebuilding in front of that line after the storm can be discouraged by denial of flood insurance and other subsidy programs.

Relocation

Active relocation is the moving of a building back before it is either threatened or damaged. *Passive relocation* is achieved by rebuilding a destroyed structure in another area, away from the shore, and out of the coastal hazard zone. Deep property lots are an important element in providing for the probability for retreat. Long-term relocations involve moving houses and villages off flood plains and nonbarrier coasts.

Setbacks

Setbacks are designed to keep structures out of extreme hazardous zones (coastal erosion, flooding, storm surges). A stringline setback simply requires that new construction be a fixed distance inland from a reference line (e.g., back of the beach, vegetation line, the crest of the sand dune).

Acquisition

Land acquisition can be an important part of a managed retreat plan. Land in the public trust—through federal, state, and local ownership—serves the public well in conservation, recreation, and tourism, providing public access to the shore, preserving aesthetics, and protecting the habitat. Governments have land acquisition programs and can offer tax incentives, trading of land, or transference of development rights. Most acquisitions are hampered by lack of money. California and Florida have successful programs. Just how well a publicly owned coastline can serve its citizens is demonstrated by Chicago's 18 miles of continuous park on the south shore of Lake Michigan.

Avoidance

The best way not to experience a hazard is to avoid it. It would seem that a discriminating house builder would avoid building near specific hazards, critical habitats, or sediment sources. Often people take chances in order to gain a better view and be closer to the action. But if the disincentive is a lack of insurance coverage, they may be persuaded to follow a more cautious plan.

Managed Retreat at Work: Nags Head, North Carolina

Nags Head, North Carolina, has adopted building standards more restrictive than required by the Federal Emergency Management Agency (FEMA) or the North Carolina Coastal Area Management program. Incentives are used to encourage development to be located as far from the ocean as possible (a minimum 150 feet from mean high tide water). Deep lots running perpendicular to shore provide considerable room for expansion. Before rebuilding after a storm, Nags Head may require adjacent lots to join as single lots in common ownership. New construction of wood frame, multistory, multifamily buildings is not permitted. There are strict limits on the amounts of impervious surfaces allowed within oceanfront property.

The general theme of Nags Head's mitigation plan is based on a strategy of recognized history and the assumption that it is far better to adapt a policy of planned retreat than to wait for a disaster to strike. For example, one landmark property in Nags Head is called the Outlaw House. It has been moved back five times in 100 years. A beach replenishment project would cost $9,000,000 for sand replenishment for 4.5 miles, compared with a retreat option of $2,000,000 every 20–25 years.

The Need for Long-term Managed Retreat

It is unrealistic to expect to hold the line of rising seawater against the world's developed coastlines. Managed retreat provides the best set of tools for alleviating hazards and reducing property damage. Avoidance is the best solution for undeveloped and lightly settled areas, while various forms of relocation are the best long-term solutions for urbanized coastal zones. Coastal land acquisition is one method for meeting both of these goals, although much greater funding will be needed. Setbacks are temporary solutions, even when defined as rolling setbacks. In order for relocation to work, land-use planning and zoning efforts will have to take a holistic approach. For example, barrier island management policies must consider the entire island. The manager must grasp both the site-specific problems and the entire island perspective.

Activity

Managed retreat is the inevitable outcome of coastal management. As the seas rise, as the populations of coastal sites swell, as the insurance rates become prohibitively high, and as government aid to the homeless diminishes, the fact becomes obvious. We will have to retreat from the beach.

The nature of this retreat from every beach or coastal site will be different. The retreat will depend on the nature of the site, the traditions of the community, the rate of ocean advance and erosion, and the population density.

Imagine you have the task of managing the retreat from a privately owned beach along the ocean or a great lake. Consider what you have to do to organize the entire community to plan a retreat from the oceanfront to a site secure from the ravages of the sea for the next 50 years. Consider all variables in getting the people of the community to agree to the retreat and to the cost involved.

How can the ideas of managed retreat work at this shoreline? Is the shore threatened by destruction within 50 years? Are the citizens amenable to managed retreat? Can engineering preserve the beach and coastline? What strategies of retreat do you think might work?

For Further Reading

Committee on Engineering Implications of Changes in Relative Mean Sea Level. 1987. *Responding to changes in sea level*. Washington, DC: National Academy Press.

Howard, J. D. 1985. Strategy for beach preservation proposed. Adapted from a position paper from the second Skidway Institute of Oceanography Conference on America's Eroding Shoreline, Savannah, GA. *Geotimes* (December).

Neal, W. J. et.al. In Press. Managed retreat. In Schwartz, M., ed. *Encyclopedia of coastal science*. Dordrecht, Netherlands: Kluwer Academic Publishers.

Townsend, M. 2002. Sea set to claim England's coastal treasures. *The Observer* (December 22).

Managed Retreat: How Does It Work?

G o to a beach and see how the waves and the beach interact. Search for signs of erosion on the beach and the coastal structure. Look for the tidal levels: high tide, low tide, and medium high tide. Look for signs of recent high tide damage, storm damage, and advancing sea damage. Ask local residents to describe the history of storm-wave damage to the coastal environment. As far back as the oldest resident remembers, where were the tide lines? What other coastal features tell about the past? Are there signs of abandoned structures overtaken by the sea?

Find out what protective engineering measures the residents undertook to hold the sea back from the land. These may include any of the following:

PhotoDisc

1. Parallel to the shore, an above water *breakwater* to reduce wave height at the shoreline is a popular and effective control of beach erosion.

2. *Sea walls* are built above high tide, facing the sea. They withstand topping, but a large amount of water to the rear of the wall causes a significant amount of scoring and erosion that, in turn, can cause a backwash of the wall.

3. A *bulkhead* is like a wall, except it arms the face of cliffs with impermeable rock to protect the softer rock of the cliff. With constant beating by the surf it, too, fails by back washing out the cliff behind the wall.

4. *Revetments* consist of loose interlocking units laid on a slope to some point on the profile of the upper beach. They serve the same function as a sea wall or a bulkhead.

5. A *groin* is a perpendicular structure that extends into the water, serves to limit the offshore current and block the ac-

cumulation of sediment. It is effective for about 50 years.

6. The *vegetation* on the seaward side of the dunes and the sound side of the marsh has the favorable effect of reducing the chance of the soil being blown away. However, it is not effective in a hurricane.

7. *Sand replenishment* is an expensive way to retain a beach. It is only cost effective where beaches serve large populations that can pay for moving in new sand.

Holding back the sea—as water levels continue to rise—may always be technically feasible; however, it will not always be technically sound or economically practical. In areas where the long-range cost or the environmental damage due to shoreline stabilization is exorbitant, it will be prudent to move back from the shore. Planned retreat requires years of preparation. A retreat can occur as a gradual process, or as catastrophic land abandonment.

NATIONAL SCIENCE TEACHERS ASSOCIATION

To Hunt or Not to Hunt

Evidence from the fossil record suggests that humans have been hunters for about 3 million years. *The Hunting Hypothesis,* by Robert Ardrey, describes our ancestors as meat-eating apes who hunted in packs like wolves, using lethal weapons. Over 99 percent of human history was hunting-dependent. Cultures attached a high value to hunting skills because by natural selection, those who were best at hunting were also the most likely to survive.

In the 19th century, hunting turned into a different enterprise. It was neither a primary method of obtaining food, nor even a sport. Hunting became a business to control the world food market. In the process, market hunters disrupted market systems by destroying large carnivores such as mountain lions and wolves. They also killed off herds of bison to subjugate the Indians and to replace wildlife with high-yield crops and livestock.

PhotoDisc

At the beginning of the 20th century, when the populations of many species of game animals were at an all-time low, many sportsmen who loved to hunt realized they must accept the stewardship for wildlife in the United States or lose their heritage. The sport-hunting public, led by Teddy Roosevelt, Aldo Leopold, and John James Audubon, initiated a conservation effort that included passing laws to save many species of wildlife from being totally lost to future generations.

A series of acts, including the Lacey (bird import, 1900), the Migratory Bird Treaty (1918), the Duck Stamp (1918), and the Dingell-Johnson (fishing, 1950), placed non-migratory game management under the control of the states, eliminating market hunting for most species. Income from licenses and migratory waterfowl stamps provided a funding base that now exceeds $450 million per year. The purchase of land designated for wildlife and the development of scientifically based game management were intended to benefit game and other wildlife.

Today, hunting remains closely linked to game management. Many species are managed specifically to provide quality hunting. Some species (such as the ring-necked pheasant and partridge) have been added to existing habitats for hunters, and others (such as wild turkeys) have been restored in areas where they once disappeared. Major portions of the budgets of state natural resources departments come from hunters, and go to management of game.

Modern hunting is embroiled in a major controversy. There are approximately 14 million hunters confronting an indeterminate number of animal rights activists who are attempting to have hunting banned in the United States. The two groups are polarized. Confrontations are occurring in the courts, the state legislatures, the U.S. Congress, and the field. Those opposed to hunting challenge the right of people to kill game

animals, the legality of the funding base, and the use of hunting as a game management tool. However, the core of their concern with hunting is the morality of the sport.

Are Humans Hunters by Nature?

Yes, say pro-hunting sportspersons. Hunting is our heritage and an integral part of some peoples' interaction with nature, enhancing their enjoyment of the outdoors. Over 14 million Americans seek this type of challenge, and attempt to learn the complex relationships in nature that affect hunting success.

Anti-hunting activists disagree. While humans probably evolved for several hundred thousand generations when hunting skills were necessary for survival, the activists say that the perpetuation of ancestral behaviors isn't justified. Modern humans certainly do not condone warfare, cannibalism, or suppression of women just because those behaviors existed in the past.

Is Hunting a Necessary Game Management Tool?

Anti-hunting people say no. They deny that hunting is required for wild game management. Many game animals undergo natural fluctuations in population size without any interference from humans. The hunter is accused of killing the genetically strong rather than the less fit and thus changing the gene pool of the species.

Hunters disagree. They argue that nature must supply a surplus to ensure the survival of the species, and as many as 80 percent die each year, many from starvation. Furthermore, in the case of deer and elk, the habitats in which they live have often changed dramatically. For example, reduction in woodland has resulted in

Photo courtesy of James Mulhern and James Mulhern, Jr.

far more deer in the upper Midwest than in the previous century. Hunters deny that they exert a reverse-selection pressure, since they usually shoot the first animal they can find, which may often be a genetically inferior one. They also cite experiments at other types of population control, such as in the Everglades, which were not successful. Hunters also argue that it is better for an animal to die from a quick shot than from starvation.

Do Hunters Control the Wildlife Refuges?

National wildlife refuges were originally set up as "inviolate sanctuaries" for all living species. While duck stamp revenues do support management programs there, more than 95 percent

of the 89 million acres of refuge lands were purchased with tax dollars derived from sources unrelated to hunting. Since Congress opened large areas of our National Wildlife Refuge System to hunting in the 1960s, pro-hunting sources claim that improved management of many species of game has been documented.

Is Hunting Moral?

There are many who insist that caring, civilized people should not hunt sentient animals for fun, trophy, or sport because of the trauma, suffering, and death that result, and that a society that characterizes wild animals as "game" denies respect for life.

The pro-hunting faction finds the argument that it is immoral to kill wild game, while it is morally acceptable to destroy their habitat in order to grow crops and livestock for slaughter, to be inconsistent. In contrast, they say that hunters are thoughtful predators, who feel sadness at taking a life but still accept the natural role that humans have in nature.

Do Anti-hunting Persons Have the Right to Deny Hunters Their Right to Hunt?

Most hunters no longer have an economic need to hunt. Quick, clean slaughters by professional butchers now provide healthy meat both economically and efficiently. Therefore anti-hunting activists feel they have both the right and the duty to pursue legislation to protect wildlife and ecosystems from violence and disruption.

In contrast, the hunter does not believe that one group of citizens has a right in a free society to deny another group their heritage and historical pursuit of happiness when it does not impinge on the freedom of others. They call the activists' claims that hunters are interfering with natural ecosystems unsubstantiated, and instead insist that it was the hunters who accepted responsibility to protect wildlife at the beginning of the 20th century and continue to support management today. Furthermore, there is a hint of hypocrisy seen by hunters in those who would deny this right, but continue to eat meat and wear animal products.

For Further Reading

Ardrey, R. 1976. *The hunting hypothesis.* 1st ed. New York: H. Wolf.

Hillis, R. November 1996. Hunting and the anti's. Available online at *www. telusplanet.net/public/arrows/home_ chptr1.htm.*

Lapierre, M. September 12, 2003. *On the anti-hunting point of view.* Available online at *www. backcountryjournal.com/antihunt.htm.*

Palczak, S. Anti-hunters information page. Available online at *http://expage.com/ antihuntersinfosite.*

Watt, N. July 1, 2003. "Seize the moment" rallying cry to anti-hunting MPs. *The Guardian.* Available online at: *www. guardian.co.uk/hunt/Story/0,2763, 988539,00.html.*

Note

For various and continuing publications on hunting, contact the Humane Society of the United States, 2100 L Street NW, Washington, DC 20037, or Wildlife Conservation Fund of America, 50 West Broad Street, Columbus, Ohio 43215.

Should Modern Humans Hunt?

Hunters' View

Hunting is a sport for men and women who use their historical rights to stalk and shoot game for food and trophy as part of their cherished outdoor experience.

Such hunters as Teddy Roosevelt and John Audubon began wildlife management. Contrary to what anti-hunting activists claim, game management is currently and primarily supported by hunters' license fees and special taxes on arms and ammunition. Since conservation-minded hunters have supported wildlife programs, the number of wild animals has increased.

In the natural state, populations of wildlife tend to increase and decrease in cycles. Humans, however, have changed so much of the natural environment for our own use that the natural cycles for wildlife are no longer a constant. Thus, animals such as deer often die slowly in agony from hunger, cold, or disease frequently caused by overpopulation in a restricted environment. Hunters harvest animals under the control of wildlife scientists. Tranquil-

Getty Images

izer guns are totally ineffective for hunting because of their short range.

Many hunters are concerned citizens who work for the maintenance of abundant and healthy wildlife. In a free society, their historical right to hunt must never be denied by anti-hunting activists with different moral values.

Photo courtesy of James Mulhern and James Mulhern, Jr.

Anti-hunting Activists' View

Sport hunting of wildlife is a recreational pastime where hunters derive pleasure from stalking and shooting mammals and birds that are sensitive to pain and have a right to live in the natural environment.

Most funds for the purchase and maintenance of wilderness land come from general taxes. The payment of special taxes and the purchase of duck stamps do not of themselves carry rights to hunt on land purchased for wildlife refuges.

Population fluctuation has not always been common in species. Natural populations do not require humans to stabilize their sizes. When hunters harvest game animals, they usually go for trophy specimens—the genetically strong rather than the small and weak. When necessary, excess populations should be harvested by professional biologists using painless tranquilizers and lethal injections.

Hunting is a violent blood sport that has lost its original purpose, and now serves only to entertain hunters who kill and wound the fittest wildlife.

Questions to Consider

1 When game management fails to produce stable populations of such wildlife as deer,

should government game specialists harvest the surplus rather than invite sport hunters onto the refuge to track and shoot the animals?

2 To what extent should the law permit or prevent an anti-hunting activist to disrupt a hunter in the field?

3 Is there a moral difference between killing a wild animal for food and raising an animal in captivity for slaughter?

4 Is it fair or unreasonable to ban hunting, thereby causing loss of funding for game management, loss of funds for habitat purchase and maintenance, and economic hardship for supply and sporting equipment companies?

5 What kind of compromise would you suggest for the hunter and the anti-hunting activist?

6 Can a person have a reverence for nature and wild animals even though he or she hunts?

A Closer Look at the Lottery

I n 1964, there was one legal state lottery—in the state of New Hampshire. In 1971, there were three legal state lotteries (in New Hampshire, New York and New Jersey), and one lottery in the province of Quebec. By 2000, a state lottery was legal in 36 states and the District of Columbia. Today casinos operate in 26 states. Some form of gambling is now legal in every state except Utah and Hawaii.

Getty Images

FIGURE 9

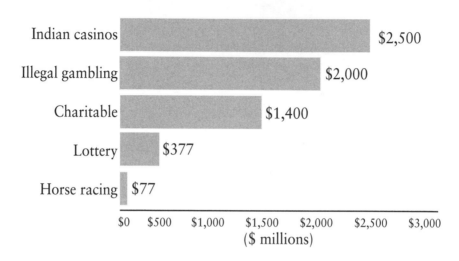

Estimated wagering in Minnesota in 2002

Indian casinos $2,500

Illegal gambling $2,000

Charitable $1,400

Lottery $377

Horse racing $77

$0 $500 $1,000 $1,500 $2,000 $2,500 $3,000
($ millions)

SOURCE (MINNESOTA STATE LOTTERY 2002)

How did this proliferation occur in just 40 years? Why did the state legislatures vote to permit gambling interests to conduct numbers games under the protection of the state? Was it because gambling became legal and moral? Was it because the state could control the betting and the distribution of the profits? Did the citizens believe the promise that the winner would pocket the prizes (50 percent), the lottery committee would charge the state for printing, advertising, administration, and retailing, (17 percent), and the state beneficiaries would take the remaining share (33 percent)?

The reality in 2004 has changed. The lotteries in Washington State include Lotto, Mega America, Quinto, Keno, The Daily Game, Lucky for Life, and Scratch. In Minnesota (see Figure 9), the lottery take is $377 million a year, charitable gambling takes in $1.4 billion each year, illegal gambling takes $2 billion a year, the casi-

nos take an estimated $2.5 billion a year, and horse racing takes in $77 million a year. There are 217 Indian tribes running casino operation in 342 gambling operation in 28 states. The only form of gambling under the control of the state and to which the profits accrue for the state is the lotteries. Let us examine this form of gambling, compare its profits with private gambling enterprises, and search for the true worth of this mechanism of paying the state treasury.

The Contests

The lottery has taken on multiple forms with the advent of the computer. In the first form, the lottery (Lotto) may be a ticket with a series of six numbers of one through forty. The numbers can be drawn at random by the computer, or the numbers can be chosen by hand in a televised event. Each $1 lottery ticket contains two sets of six numbers, for example, one ticket may have the numbers 3, 8, 14, 25, 27, 40. If a person matches say X 8 X X 27 40, he may win $3 for getting three numbers correct. If all six numbers match, the prize may b   e $1 million. With each draw of six numbers of the lottery, the chance of winning the big prize is 1: 6,991,908. To spice up the chances of winning, the numbers are changed to a deck of cards, and the player "draws" five cards that match the 52 cards in a deck; for example 3♣, 7♦, 10♦, J♥, A♠. The contestant will win the grand prize of no less than $300,000—because he is playing only five cards in a 52-card deck. The games go on following the same format. The odds of winning five of five are 1: 2,598,960. A game can become more difficult to win when the sixth row becomes a red bar and the numbers look like this: 7, 23, 25, 33, 40, 3. In the first round of this contest, the chance of winning is 1: 11,069,877. The odds of winning this lottery are intensely higher. Winning $3 for three, $20 for four, and $5,000 for five numbers do not compare with winning $l million for all six of the numbers. Each time no one wins, the grand prize rises by about a $1 million.

States have a monopoly on the lottery. In the state of Georgia, for example, the private management of running video poker or the running of numbers is outlawed. Georgia fines and imprisons anyone who breaks these laws. The state claims unregulated video poker or playing numbers is addictive and causes financial ruin. The state makes a fortune off of gambling, but does not make a dime off of video poker and the numbers. The result is that private video poker and numbers are outlawed, but the state lottery runs as a big business. In a nearby state, video poker is legal and the state may get its cut. To declare that private forms of gambling are dangerous and immoral—but that state-run gambling is moral—is a scary proposition.

The considerable growth of legalized gambling in the last 10 years has certainly changed the nature of gaming in America. In 1992 in Rhode Island, gambling money from the state lottery made up just 1.4 percent of the state's general budget. In fiscal year 2003, gambling money accounted for 11 percent of general revenues, for a total of $320 million. Gambling money is now an essential source of state funding and it is becoming difficult to conceive of a state budget without an increasing supply of gaming income. Big money in gambling lies with the casinos. Many states are voting in the 2004 election on the issue of casino operations. States are now setting their sights on the casinos.

Nevertheless, state revenues from gambling currently arise from just one source—state lotteries. Note how the estimated wagering in Washington for year 2002 is distributed (Figure 10).

Distribution of Lottery Money in Washington State

The Washington lottery over 20 years has produced $1.8 billion for the state general fund, $83.4 million for education, $21.8 million for the Seattle Mariners baseball stadium, and $25.5 million for the Seattle Seahawks football stadium. In most states the contribution to education is dominant but it is not always used in the same way. In some states, the fund provides for college scholarships. In other states, lottery proceeds provide capital funds for school building, before- and after-school funds, general education funds, and so on. In some states the funds go into the general school revenue fund from which they are distributed depending upon need. There is no specified use for the funds.

Figure 10

Where lottery money went for FY2002 in Washington State

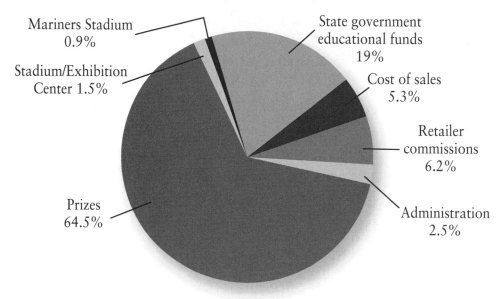

Mariners Stadium
0.9%

State government
educational funds
19%

Stadium/Exhibition
Center 1.5%

Cost of sales
5.3%

Retailer
commissions
6.2%

Prizes
64.5%

Administration
2.5%

SOURCE (WASHINGTON STATE LOTTERY 2002)

In general, the distribution of revenues from the sale of lottery tickets follows the pattern of 50 percent to the winners of prizes, 17 percent for administrative expenses and 33 percent for education.

Gambling Fever Grows

While governor of Montana, Marc Racicot said, "Once we legalize any form of gambling, it is nearly always impossible to go back. And we should always remember that when we subscribe to the fiction that we can get something for nothing, in truth, we nearly always get nothing for something." The blight of gambling addiction includes declaring bankruptcy, needing to take out loans, "maxing out" credit accounts, embezzling at work, writing bad

checks, and committing insurance fraud. The social cost of gambling greatly exceeds the profits of gambling won by the states. Relating statistics to support his remarks, Racicot urged lawmakers of Montana not to expand its current level of gambling.

The National Gambling Impact Study Commission, studying the booming market from 1976 to the present, was not able to say whether the phenomenon was an economic boom or an economic disaster. The commission was composed of a diverse group of people and they were not able to reach a final conclusion that praised or condemned the phenomena. Gambling has grown in every dimension throughout America. State-sponsored lotteries, Indian casinos, private casinos, illegal gambling, charitable gambling, Internet gaming, horse racing, and other efforts all vie to separate the cash from the risk taker. If the lid is coming off all inhibitions to gambling, where will it end? If the governor of Montana and other like-minded administrators cannot prevail in curbing gambling of all kinds, to whom can we turn? Or is this a freedom that must run itself out? Shall we gamble on the odds of getting something for nothing, until we all get nothing for something?

Questions for Discussion

■ Let's concern ourselves with the 37 state-sponsored lotteries, paying out 50 percent in million dollar prizes (with more than 50 percent of that going to the IRS), 17 percent in administration costs, and 33 percent into state revenues, mostly education. Is it worth it?

■ Would it be better to divide up the prize into ten biweekly prizes of $100 thousand each, thus spreading the wealth around?

■ What is the purpose of allowing the single prize to progress to $40 million in 20 weeks, while allowing no one to win a prize?

■ Is a grand prize of millions of dollars so intense an incentive that it trumps the lesser prizes, and focuses the players on the one big prize—so large that the winner cannot comprehend it?

■ What lesson do we teach by dividing the lottery pie of $100 million into $50 million to the winner ($25 million prize money plus $25 million federal income taxes), $17 million for administration, and $33 million for revenue for the state?

For Further Reading

Boswell, E. September 13, 1997. Governor opposes expansion of gambling in Montana. *MSU-Bozeman Communications Services.* Available online at *www.montana.edu/wwwpb/univ/gamble.html.*

Brisman, A. 1999. *American Mensa guide to casino gambling: Winning ways.* New York: Sterling Publishing Company.

Minnesota State Lottery: Lottery Overview. Available online at: *www.lottery.state.mn.us/overview.*

Weiss, A. E. 1991. *Lotteries: Who wins, who loses?* Berkeley Heights, NJ: Enslow Publishers, Inc.

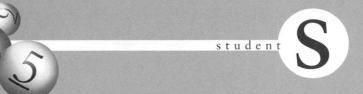

The Lottery: Is It Really Worth It?

Getty Images

Since 1976, in nearly every state in America, gambling has been growing steadily. Today there is gambling of every conceivable type in nearly every conceivable place. There are the lotteries sponsored by the state, Indian casinos, illegal gambling, charitable gambling, horse races, private casinos, Internet gambling, and more. The states are facing serious budget deficits, and state-sponsored lotteries are under pressure to increase their revenue and squeeze as much money as they can from the players. Now state governors are looking at casinos, which take in a massive amount of money. State-sponsored casino gambling may be just around the corner. In the meantime, state-sponsored lotteries are an increasing force on the market. Thirty-six states and the District of Columbia have legalized the lottery, now broadly defined to include most kind of computer-controlled gambling.

Anyone over 21 (or in some states, 18) can buy numbers at odds of 1 to millions and then wait for the announcement on radio, on television, and in newspapers of the winning number. The chances are that you have not won, but in the unlikely event you have won a large amount, you must go the state lottery headquarters for the award. There, officials deduct the income tax and give you a check either for the amount due or for the amount prorated over a period of years. Of the remaining prize amount, 17 percent is paid for the expenses of running the lottery and 33 percent goes into state funds as a contribution from you.

Questions to Consider

1 Is it worth the anticipation, the thrill, and the disappointment to risk a few dollars against the great odds to win a million or more dollars?

2 When we surrender to the notion that the lottery gives us something for nothing, how long does it take to realize that nearly always we really get nothing for something?

3 Gambling has its benefits. It gives back money to the state and people enjoy it as a form of recreation. It allows for escape, risk-taking, and social interaction. But these benefits extract a high price. The social cost is significant to those who lose big in gambling. The more society gambles, the greater the incidence of poverty. Suppose the benefits of gambling were (1) greater than the costs of gam-

FIGURE 11

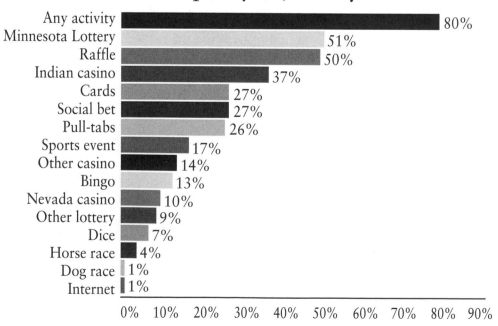

"In the past year, have you bet on...?"

Activity	Percent
Any activity	80%
Minnesota Lottery	51%
Raffle	50%
Indian casino	37%
Cards	27%
Social bet	27%
Pull-tabs	26%
Sports event	17%
Other casino	14%
Bingo	13%
Nevada casino	10%
Other lottery	9%
Dice	7%
Horse race	4%
Dog race	1%
Internet	1%

SOURCE (MINNESOTA STATE LOTTERY 2002)

bling, (2) less than the costs of gambling, or (3) equal to the cost of gambling. What benefits of gambling do you find acceptable?

4　State officials can avoid dependence on gambling, and find alternative sources of funding. How would you revise the system?

5　Is winning a large amount of money such a desirable goal? Many lottery winners turned winning into disaster, both socially and financially. Research some of the problems that have occurred in the lives of lottery winners.

6　"In the past year, have you bet on …?" Notice in the chart (Figure 11) that the Minnesota menu of betting events lists 16 activities in 2002. Eighty percent of Minnesotans indicated they placed a bet in 2002. Fifty-one percent indicated that they bet at least once on the Minnesota lottery, and one percent placed a bet on the Internet. How do you account for the fact that 51 percent of Minnesotans bet on the Minnesota Lottery, yet only $377 million was bet on the state-sponsored lottery while $6,354 million was bet on all gambling activities in 2002?

Index

*Page numbers in **boldface** type refer to figures.*

Index

F

Federal Emergency Management Agency
     (FEMA), 47
Fölling, Asbjorn, 34
Fragile-X syndrome, screening for, 38

G

GA (tabun), 22, **23**
Gambling. *See* Lottery
Game management, 52–53, 56–57. *See also*
     Hunting
Garrod, Archibald, 33
Genetic screening, 33–38
     access to information from, 38
     discussion questions about, 34–35, 38
     goals of, 34
     of high-risk ethnic groups, 35
     history of, 33–34
     mandatory, 34, 35
     neonatal, 34, 38
     premarital, 34
     student lesson on, 37–38
     voluntary, 34
Geneva protocols, 22
Greenhouse effect, 46
Groin, for coastal management, 50
Gurden, John, 3
Guthrie, Robert, 34

H

Hubble telescope, 28
Hunt, Cordell, 24
Hunting, 51–57
     anti-hunting activists' view of, 52, 54, 56
     discussion questions about, 56–57
     for game management, 52–53
     history of, 51–52
     hunters' view of, 54, 55
     legislation regarding, 52
     morality of, 53–54, 57
     in national wildlife refuges, 53
     student lesson on, 55–57
Hydrogen cyanide, 22
Hypothyroidism, screening for, 34, 38

I

International Space Station, 29
Iraq war of 2003, 21

J

Johnson, Jeffrey G., 39

K

Kass, Leon, 17

L

Leopold, Aldo, 52
Lottery, 59–67
     benefits of gambling, 66–67
     discussion questions about, 63, 66–67
     distribution of funds from
          (Washington State), 61–62, **62,** 66
     estimated wagering on, 60, **60**
     gambling fever and, 62–63, **66**
     growth of legalized gambling, 59–60, 61, 65
     state monopoly on, 61
     student lesson on, 65–67
     types of contests, 60–61
LSD-25, 26

M

Mace (chloroacetophenone), 22, **23,** 26
Mammals, cloning of, **3,** 4, 5
Managed retreat for coastal management, 45–50
     by abandonment, 46–47
     activity related to, 48
     by avoidance, 47
     definition of, 46
     engineering solutions for, 46, 49–50
     hurricane damage and, 45–46
     by land acquisition, 47
     long-term need for, 48
     at Nags Head, North Carolina, 47–48
     by relocation, 47
     setbacks for, 47

Index

T

Tabun (GA), 22, **23**
Tay-Sachs disease, screening for, 34, 35
Tear gas, 22, **23**
Television viewing. *See* Violence in media
Temple, Stanley, 8
Thalassemia, screening for, 35
Tularemia, 24

V

V-chip technology, 44
Violence in media, 39–44
    aggressive behavior related to viewing of,
        39–40, 43
    cartoon portrayal of, 41–42
    desensitizing effect of, 40
    discussion questions about, 40–42
    freedom of speech and, 44
    frequency of exposure to, 40, 43–44
    imitation of, 40
    "mean world syndrome" and, 40
    responsible vs. irresponsible portrayal of, 40
    student lesson on, 43–44
    v-chip technology and, 44
    viewing by children, 40, 41–42, 44
VX, 22, 25

W

Weapons of mass destruction. *See* Chemical
    and biological weapons
Weather satellites, 28
Wells, H. G., 22–23
Wilmut, Ian, 4